無限 STEEL SUPER 上鋼

2014
高雄國際鋼雕藝術節
Kaohsiung International Steel
& Iron Sculpture Festival

共同主辦

高雄市政府文化局
Bureau of Cultural Affairs Kaohsiung City Government

財團法人東和鋼鐵文化基金會
Tung Ho Steel Foundation

目錄
Contents

「無限上鋼」高雄國際鋼雕藝術節
About KISISF

在高雄，鋼鐵不只是工業材料，它奠定了一座城市的產業基礎，煉就出在地居民的堅毅性格，更轉化成最具代表性的藝術形態與創作熱力。

2002 年，高雄開始舉辦以城市產業特質為主題的高雄國際鋼雕藝術節，將鋼鐵冰冷生硬的特質，以藝術形式賦予新的語意，讓鋼鐵不再只是一門產業，一種材料。

每兩年一度的鋼雕藝術節，創辦至今已進入第七屆，以鋼雕現地創作營為主軸，邀請國內外鋼雕藝術家到高雄進行創作，強化環境、藝術家、創作行為與民眾互動的關聯性，焊接的火力、材料的運用、戶外創作的體力與耐力、作品突破性的思考與創意，都讓跟著藝術家一同經歷創作的民眾回味不已。

在 2014 年的高雄國際鋼雕藝術節以「無限上鋼」為主題，試圖呈現鋼鐵雕塑的無限可能，歐亞六位重量級藝術家齊聚於駁二場域，進行一場藝術、鋼鐵與港口的對話。在創作營的藝術家名單中，有一半以上邀請自國外，分別來自義大利、俄羅斯、日本、中國，強化了本屆的國際性與世界觀。在作品噸位上，更是超越過往現場創作營的巔峰，財團法人東和鋼鐵文化基金會特別挹注了 120 噸的鋼鐵，讓每位藝術家可以運用 20 噸的鋼材進行大型創作。

如果說 2012 的鋼雕，是為高雄在柴山下海港邊，沿著百年鐵道打造了一座氣勢磅礴的鋼雕公園，那麼，2014 的鋼雕，便是在碼頭上船舶前強力飆焊，在水岸的海天裡創造最不可限量的鋼雕地景。

To Kaohsiung, steel and iron are more than building materials, they are the foundation of the entire city whose population is described as iron-willed. Their iron-willedness is the origin of their passion to arts.

Inaugurated in 2002, the Kaohsiung International Steel & Iron Sculpture Festival emphasizes the relation between the industry and the city. However cold and hard, these industrial materials could be given new significance through art forms.

KISISF takes place every two years, 2014 was the 7th Festival. KISISF invites local and foreign sculptors to work on-site so they will pay attention to their role in the environment, including their creation and interactions with the public. Being able to participate with the work of the artists, the public is always amazed by the fire of wielding, the application of materials, the unexpected art expression, as well as the stamina and patience of artists who work in the workshop and present their projects outdoors.

The theme of the 2014 KISISF was "Steel Super", an attempt to explore the seeming unlimited possibilities of steel and iron. Six artists from Asia and Europe gathered in the Pier-2 to communicate with the harbor and the city with their art of steel and iron. In addition to Taiwanese artists, artists from Italy, Russia, Japan and China have broadened the perspective of 2014 KISISF. The total weight of their works have broken the records of the past, indicating that the artists have reached their climax of creation. Thanks to the 120 tons steel and iron sponsored by the Tung Ho Steel Foundation, each artist had as much as 20 tons at his disposal.

The 2012 KISISF has constructed a grand sculpture park along the one-hundred-year old railway, and the 2014 KISISF has, in front of the harbored boats, laid out a ceaseless steel sculpture landscape between the water and the sky.

序

高雄國際鋼雕藝術節：鋼鐵城市的藝術使命

雖然高雄並不出產製成鋼鐵的礦砂，但卻是台灣有名的鋼鐵之城。日據時期起，打狗鹽埕便開啟了台灣鐵工所的煉鐵運作，許多製糖與鐵道運輸設備都由台灣鐵工所製作，成為台灣工業的推手。而高雄經濟的起步，更有賴鋼鐵廠奠定基石，鋼鐵的重要性使其成為足以代表高雄城市的產業。

於是，我們自 2002 年起，便開始辦理高雄國際鋼雕藝術節，企圖以藝術重現鋼鐵的不同樣貌，同時藉以帶出勞動階層的拚搏與堅毅。在高雄國際鋼雕藝術節這樣的國際性藝術活動中，可以看見不同地域國界不同文化背景的藝術家，努力地想融入高雄的環境與歷史，企圖運用廢鋼材創造一件與在地緊密連結的作品。這段過程十分精采與動人，因為大型鋼雕創作單靠藝術家本人無法達成，這也映照出勞動專業技術協同藝術創作以發揮最大能量。

從 2002 年到 2014 年，經歷了七屆的高雄國際鋼雕藝術節，回顧過往也可以窺見出高雄城市的變化，其中尤其以各種型態的文化活動與設計建築活絡了高雄港區，此次鋼雕創作營特地選於駁二藝術特區淺三碼頭舉辦，船舶港口成為最美的背景，更加深了場域所賦予的意涵。而在面臨城市新舊產業的時代轉換過程中，鋼鐵雕塑的現地創作也成為一種以藝術詮釋與保留文化特色的無限可能與必要途徑。

高雄市 市長

陳 菊

The Kaohsiung International Steel and Iron Sculpture Festival: The Art Mission of the City of Steel and Iron

Kaohsiung does not produce iron ore, but is known as a city of steel and iron in Taiwan. The first ironworks opened in the Yencheng area of Takao during the Japanese Occupation. It became a main manufacturer of sugar and railroad transportation equipment, and further the driving force behind heavy industry in Taiwan. Steel and iron industry on which Kaohsiung's economy is founded has been a symbol of the city.

This gave us the initiative to organize the Kaohsiung International Steel and Iron Sculpture Festival (KISISF) in 2002. Our goal has been to artistically reinterpret steel and iron, while highlighting the diligence and perseverance of industrial laborers. In this international activity, artists from diverse geographical and cultural backgrounds strive to adapt themselves to the local environment and history by turning steel scraps into sculptures closely related to Kaohsiung. It is particularly awesome and moving, since large-scale steel works demand collective effort. It also illustrates how compelling the union of labor, techniques and art can be.

A review of the 7 KISISFs from 2002 to 2014 also gives us a glimpse of the evolution of Kaohsiung. Above all, the port has been invigorated by a variety of cultural activities and architectural projects. The 2014 KISISF had chosen to take place in Dock 3, the Pier-2 Art Center, to deepen the sense of location with the beauty of the port. In the city's shift from the old to the new, the on-site steel and iron sculptures have embodied the limitless possibilities to artistically reinterpret and preserve the culture of Kaohsiung.

Chen Chu
Mayor of Kaohsiung

無限上鋼，無可限量的城市地景

鋼雕對於高雄而言，是每兩年一回的期待。

鋼雕的創作現場總是生猛有力，只要看過一次就會上癮。遍地張牙舞爪的廢鋼材，不完整的切割面、各種擠壓產生的曲折、與空氣水氣作用後的鏽蝕，定睛細看，都帶著巨大能量迸發後的美感。而起起落落的吊車、鏗鏘敲擊的聲響、打磨切割的火花，每一道工序堆砌著創作的進程，也鋪陳出一幕幕精彩印象。這就是創作現場絲毫不比作品遜色的高雄國際鋼雕藝術節，包含了視覺與聽覺的特效震撼，令人期待。

自 2002 年至今，七屆的累積，每一屆的鋼雕都肩負不同時期的使命，2014「無限上鋼」，一種突破性的自我宣示，無論是尺寸、重量、藝術國界、技術團隊，都超越了過往的極限。來自歐亞六位重量級藝術家，每位以二十噸的鋼材，在廣闊的碼頭基地上，進行一場藝術、鋼鐵與港口的對話，創作五米高度以上的大型限時現地創作，若不是技術團隊的強而有力的支援，現場即時處理能力的靈活運用，都無力造就令人激賞的地景式作品。

這個城市特質取向的藝術節慶最與眾不同之處，在於抽出了產業便失去了耀眼的光芒。若沒有財團法人東和鋼鐵文化基金會提供的百噸鋼材，若沒有在地亨昌鐵材股份有限公司提供不鏽鋼材與雷射切割，若沒有實力堅強如鋼鐵般硬底子的焊工技師群，作品氣勢不會如此磅礴，高雄鋼雕便不會如此不可限量。

高雄市政府文化局 局長

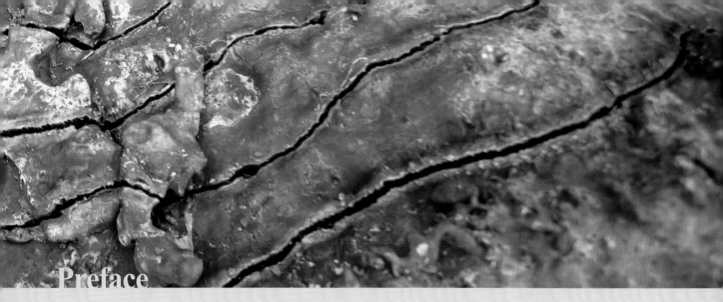

Steel Super, a Boundless Urban Landscape

Steel sculpture is a biennially expected topic in Kaohsiung.

The creation of steel sculptures is always masculine, powerful, and immediately addictive. A closer inspection of the irregular cuts, the pressed and twisted surfaces, and the rusts caused by moisture of the scattering steel scraps further reveals their vigorous beauty. The raising and lowering of cranes, the clang of steel, and the sparkles of cutting and burnishing metal that define the process of creation, are also impressive in themselves. It is this appeal comparable to that of the sculptures that characterizes the Kaohsiung International Steel and Iron Sculpture Festival (KISISF), a highly anticipated event of visual and auditory surprises.

The 7 editions of KISISFs initiated in 2002 have different missions in different times. The 2014 "Steel Super" was a call for breakthrough in size, weight, national boundary, and technical support. 6 European and Asian heavyweight artists opened a dialogue between art, steel and iron, and the harbor, by making sculptures higher than 5 meters from 20 tons of steel on-site in the spacious harbor in a limited time. Without the strong support of the technical team, its flexibility in tackling problems, the sculptures may fail to compose an admirable landscape.

Notably, the city festival would be lackluster without its industrial aspect. The grandeur of the sculptures, the boundless imagination of Kaohsiung's steel and iron, can be possible only with the 120 tons sponsored by Tung Ho Steel Foundation, the stainless steel and laser cutting service offered by Heng Chaung Iron Roofing Board Co., Ltd, and the welding technicians with an expertise as solid as steel.

Shih Che

Director-General,
Bureau of Cultural Affairs,
Kaohsiung City Government

序

藝術無限可能 鋼鐵焠煉重生

　　東和鋼鐵企業股份有限公司 1965 年於高雄設廠，高雄不僅僅是東和鋼鐵落腳的基地，也是許多同仁的故鄉，50 年來，我們對於台灣這片土地的關懷，從未停歇。

　　2002 年，高雄市政府結合產業與藝文界共同舉辦「高雄國際鋼雕藝術節」，本著對地方的特殊情感，東和鋼鐵允諾全力支持，無論是機具設備的出借，或是創作鋼材的提供，以實際行動鼓勵藝術原創。高雄國際鋼雕藝術節以文化藝術改造海港城市生活，已成為高雄市民重要的文化資產，也是本地與國際文化交流的重要對話平台。

　　2012 年東和鋼鐵成立「財團法人東和鋼鐵文化基金會」，與市府的合作規模更甚以往，國際藝術家於蓬萊倉庫廣場完成 16 件風格各異的大型鋼鐵雕塑，讓駁二藝術特區從閒置空間搖身成為鋼雕藝術新地標。今年，藝術節以「無限上鋼」為主題，邀國際藝術家挑戰 120 噸鋼材現地創作，在淺三碼頭邊創造出鋼鐵與水岸互為呼應的鋼雕地景，如今，駁二已是全台灣最具活力的新興藝文基地，其魅力來自文化長期的累積成型，本會見證其發展，實與有榮焉。

　　未來本會仍將秉持對台灣的關懷，持續致力提升國內藝文創作環境，期待鋼雕藝術是我們為城市與下一代播下的種子，讓民眾重拾對在地文化的認知，而產官學各界也在潛移默化中，開拓藝術欣賞與共同合作的新契機。

財團法人東和鋼鐵文化基金會 董事長

侯王淑昭

The Infinity of Art, the Rebirth of Steel

In 1965, Tung Ho Steel Enterprise Corporation established a plant in Kaohsiung. This city is not only a site in which locates the station of Tung Ho Steel, but also the hometown of our comrades. Our affection has been centered on this city for 50 years.

In 2002, Kaohsiung City Government cooperated with cultural and artistic field to host Kaohsiung International Steel & Iron Art Festival. By virtue of our special emotion toward this city, Tung Ho Steel dedicated to it, such as lending machines and tools to the exhibition, providing materials for artistic creation, and encouraging art creation by practical support. Kaohsiung International Steel & Iron Art Festival has reformed lives of this harbor city by culture and art, and became the essential capital asset of local citizens. In addition, it constituted an integrated international platform for cultural and creative exchange.

In 2012, Tung Ho Steel Foundation was established, and the scale of the cooperation with Kaohsiung City Government has increased. Local and foreign artists made 16 steel and iron sculptures in Penglai Area. These large-sized sculptures placed in the Pier-2 Art Center transformed the abandoned warehouse clusters into a new artistic landmark of art of steel sculpture. The theme of the 2014 Kaohsiung International Steel & Iron Art Festival was 'Steel Super'. The artists were invited to challenge site-specific art making with 120 tons of steel, and create a steel sculpture landscape along the water bank. Nowadays, The Pier-2 Art Center is one of the most vigorous artistic bases in Taiwan. Its charm springs from the accumulation of culture. It is an honor for Tung Ho Steel Foundation to witness the regeneration of the Pier-2 Art Center.

Tung Ho Steel Foundation will constantly devote ourselves in improving the art creation environment in Taiwan. We expect that the art of steel sculpture will be a motivation to lead the audiences to retrospect local culture. We also look forward to the collaboration and the appreciation of art among industry, authority and academy.

Shu-Chau Wang Ho
Chairperson of Tung Ho Steel Foundation

「無限上『鋼』」
關於 2014 高雄國際鋼雕藝術節

文／策展人　劉俊蘭（國立臺灣藝術大學雕塑學系教授）

2014 第七屆高雄國際鋼雕藝術節，以「無限上鋼」命題。馬列主義中的「無限上綱」，原指政治鬥爭過程中極度誇大其實的意識型態與批判方法，其中的「綱」，意為「原則」，確切的說，乃是「政治路線」。高雄國際鋼雕藝術節改「綱」為「鋼」，並翻轉、改變其原有的負面意涵。除了直接指明並重新思考，在以重工業奠基的高雄舉行的這個城市藝術節「鋼鐵限定」的鮮明路線與獨特屬性，更企圖以「超越既定」而「無限擴展」的創作挑戰與視野來開展這場充滿鋼鐵港都特質的藝術盛會，邀請來自義大利的 Riccardo Cordero、俄羅斯的 Nikolay Polissky、日本的前田哲明、中國的尚曉風、臺灣的梁任宏與劉柏村等六位藝術家於駁二藝術特區進行現場創作，藉其不同的觀點、殊異的藝術表現，再度擴展與鋼鐵之間超越工業的聯繫、重新刻寫與鋼鐵的新美學關係。

鋼鐵限定：
從工業物質的生產到文化的創造與革新

這屆高雄鋼雕藝術節，再度以創作營型態舉辦。常見的創作營模式，可說脫胎自奧地利藝術家 Karl Prantl 於 1959 年舉辦的「國際雕塑創作營」。Prantl 邀請藝術家進駐奧國東部荒廢的 St. Margarethen 採石場，以在地石材，進行永久設置的大型戶外雕塑創作。由某個單位或團體，邀請雕塑家到一個社區、礦場或創作基地，使用當地材料，在設定時間內公開創作，成了國際間創作營的基本典型。

然而，Prantl 立下的畢竟是石雕創作營的範例，若論採用鋼鐵為雕塑媒材者，較早的例子，可溯自 1964 年在斯洛維尼亞北部的大城 Ravne 舉辦的創作營。這個創作活動，屬於斯洛維尼亞分別於不同地點以不同材料串連進行的「造型活力」（Forma Viva）雕塑營之一。其中，受 Prantl 啟發而於 1961 年首先興辦的兩個創作營，乃是採用石材與木材，三年後，為了以較現代材料來創作造型藝術並將之融入縱橫交錯的都會空間紋理，才以北部卡林西亞地區（Koroška region）的鋼鐵工業傳統為基礎，於鋼鐵產業重鎮 Ravne 同步舉辦鋼雕創作營。

依 Prantl 模式，或更確切的說，如 Ravne 範例一般進行的「無限上鋼」創作營，同樣以地方性的物質材料——鋼鐵，特別是回收的廢鋼鐵——為創作前提。作為藝術媒介的物質材料，常有雙重性

質：召喚我們對其本身之物質性的注視，也內涵蘊意、傳達訊息而引人閱讀。藝術史學者 Thomas McEvilley 在探討晚期現代和後現代雕塑之際，曾論及一種「物質材料的圖像學」（an iconography of materials）：物質材料不只是用來觀看，也訴求於「閱讀」，「閱讀」它被採用的意義[1]。對於根植地方發展脈絡的高雄鋼雕藝術節而言，尤其是如此。

高雄乃是在鋼鐵工業中崛起：1919 年臺灣第一座鐵工廠在此設立；於太平洋戰後大量的港口沈船以及後來進口世界各地舊船的拆船工業中，港都煉鋼業進一步勃興；繼而大小鋼鐵工廠的接續發跡與立足……。鋼鐵，不僅造就工業，也形塑文化。對於今日的高雄，鋼鐵不只是項工業材料，它已深入地方的文化質理。衍生自在地工業背景的「機械總動員」特展（高雄市立美術館，2007）既嘗試以「重口味」、「草根性」……等的藝術創作，勾繪出高雄長期累積而來的直率又堅韌的社會底蘊，以及在廢五金或拆船工業中孕育的「剖肉／拼裝」的文化性格[2]。高雄的拆船廠與五金街，事實上從 1970-1980 年代左右便吸引了藝術家的注意。各式的廢鐵件，早已成為一群熱衷於鋼鐵雕塑的藝術家的材料。現實社會中的物質生產影響各個美感形式層面的這種情狀，具體展現了「文化整合」（cultural integration）的意涵，也讓人不禁聯想到廢鋼鐵雕塑（Junk Sculpture）的先驅 Richard Stankiewicz，在 1955 年時對於紐約雕塑家以廢棄物為媒材的微妙譬喻：就像南洋群島島民在他們的創造中利用貝殼一樣的自然 。[3]

「鋼鐵限定」源生並且重現高雄與鋼鐵工業密不可分的關聯，其中牽引出的，根本是整個文化脈絡。而這並不只是來自鋼鐵材料本身，也涵蓋處理材料的機具配備、團隊分工與集體協力所展現的工業特質，特別是廢鋼鐵的切割、分解、重組和焊接所折射出的港都廢五金與拆船工業的文化背景與城市歷史。

如果說記憶的意義在此有其重要性，而「無限上鋼」創作營所訴求的大型公共雕塑，也特別讓人與紀念碑的傳統相聯想，然而，「無限上鋼」卻不只是以其為靜態的醒示符碼、表徵已經深化的記憶，更關注形同某種「表演藝術」的即席創作中、當個人創作過程化為公眾藝術活動之際，集體工業記憶的「當下化」，以及重新記述與再度書寫。在創作營現場建構的鋼鐵世界氛圍裡，空間性的感知與時間性的記憶，同時延展。不僅召喚且更新對於高雄港都的記憶，也見證或說參與此鋼鐵城市從工業到後工業的轉型與文化發展。

在全球化的時代下，如此的「鋼鐵限定」，猶如一種「文化差異性」的生產方法，別具基進意義。創作營的國際參與，更企圖把具有歷史縱深的在地文化脈絡拉到國際平台去重新演繹、在地方文化中納入異質性，既刺激其中的反身觀照，也探問更新與豐厚衍化的可能，催發「文化差異」的活潑動能。總結而論，「鋼鐵限定」不只回應工業物質的生產，更根本的推促文化的創造與革新—— 不僅就地方而言是如此，就普遍的意義來說，其實亦然。

面對框限：
從侷限的突破到框架的挑戰

利用鋼鐵材料，六位藝術家，在駁二淺三碼頭，進行 18 天的即席創作 —— 以創作營模式舉行的「無限上鋼」鋼雕藝術節，除了「鋼鐵限定」，亦即「限材」之外，也「限地」乃至「限時」創作。然而，具有如此前提限制的創作營活動本身，卻也含有突破個人侷限的作用。「無限上鋼」既展演體現創作營「突破侷限」的本質意義，也進而嘗試挑戰其既定機制、現實條件以及美學概念的框架，探尋鋼鐵雕塑創作的新表現。

「限地」創作，便隱含了值得挖掘的解放與突破作用。「無限上鋼」創作營中，來自不同國度的藝術家離開自己的工作室而進駐駁二，在劃定的地點公開創作，並不能被簡化為是單純的移地工作，無法視同於印象派畫家 Claude Monet 為了種種水上風光的寫生，特意打造一艘「工作室小船」那般的「可移動的工作室」的概念。事實上，在「限地」創作的框架中啟動的，是一種根本突破工作室的藝術實踐。其中，首先觸及的是一種客觀創作條件全然改

變的「異地創作」，激發藝術家跳離慣常的表現習性、改變既定的創作前提，在突破「慣性」和「常態」的挑戰中，反芻、重省也開發自我創作經驗。同時，「限地」創作的制約，也召喚出回應在地環境的刺激與啟發而與其空間或歷史關係密切的「現地創作」（In Situ，亦譯為「因地制宜」藝術）內容，有別於工作室裡創作的作品[4]。另外，不容忽略的，創作營的「限地」創作，並且涉及藝術家的集群。受邀的藝術家們於活動現場，在創作經驗與觀點的對話中，進入集體創作激盪的狀態、催發新的敏感性與潛能，同樣也拓展了「限地」創作的開放意義。

創作往往超越個己經濟能力所及之外的大型宏偉雕塑，對藝術家而言，特別是創作營翻轉現實侷限的最具體展現。跨國創作經驗豐富的 Neal Barab 稱讚「創作營是雕塑家夢想的實現」，此乃原因之一，他甚至認為這也是 Prantl 發起創作營的動機[5]。如果說從創作營濫觴至今，設置大型雕塑作品一直都是興辦者的重要訴求，相對的，這卻提供了藝術家挑戰大型創作的機會。「無限上鋼」不但把創作營的這個可能性，充分展現，並且更進一步地，突破之前鋼雕藝術節的作品尺寸規格，支援藝術家創作至

少五米高的大型雕塑。在完成的作品中，尚曉風的雕塑高達六米三，劉柏村所創作的，長度與高度甚至超過九米。

在創作營期間完成如此的大型雕塑，也確實推演了「限時」創作的可能性。其中的執行與實踐，工事浩大。「無限上鋼」以現場完備而到位的配備與技術團隊——吊車、堆高機、高空作業車與各式必要機具，特別是總數達 26 名的助手以及 2 名配電人員，為投入大規模創作的藝術家提供協力。首度的，本屆鋼雕藝術節透過列名紀錄，為這些在地的合作者留下了參與的軌跡：包括執行總監蔡坤霖、技術統籌鄭陽晟，以及由蘇建寅先生領軍的助手群。這種「類工程」的創作過程，體現的不僅是藝術家「統合性」的創造力，也是大型鋼鐵雕塑中集體合作、勞力密集的「勞動美學」。

一般雕塑創作營的作品規格，五公尺以上的其實較為罕見。「無限上鋼」創作營得以限時即席地完成如此的大型雕塑，與鋼鐵材料的本質密切相關：藉助切割與焊接等工業技術，鋼鐵易於堆砌、組合，可以直接構作，快速、自發甚至具有可逆性。「無限上鋼」中的大型創作，不僅再次展演更企圖重新探索鋼鐵有別於其他雕塑材料之即時與直接的媒介特性與構成潛能。

大尺寸規格的創作不僅臨場演繹鋼鐵雕塑特質，也讓藝術家得以經營作品與觀眾之間不僅訴諸視覺也邀請身體互動的活潑關係。就如劉柏村和前田哲明在此次創作營所完成的《雲端漫步》和《無題2015——高雄》，觀眾不只是繞行觀看，也得以信步穿梭、進入駐足，在開放的大型作品空間中感受與體驗。

雕塑的尺寸規格，常取決於它被設定的背景，因而也牽動作品與其所在之環境空間的關係，並影響著它可能負載的意義與發揮的功能。1988 年，Claes Oldenburg 在談及他誇張放大日常生活物件的巨型公共雕塑時提到：「我們為實用的私人物件注入了建築性的功能，我們使之與接受它的場所相連結。」[6] 也正如 Florence de Mèredieu 晚近對「空間的構築」（L'architecture de l'espace）所進行的探討中所顯示的，不僅 Oldenburg 的作品，許多藝

術家——就如 Louise Nevelson、Jean Dubuffet 等等——的大型戶外雕塑，都見證了大尺寸規格得以促使雕塑與環境空間建立積極關係的效能：介入、對照、連結或融合，乃至於進一步地進行構築。Nevelson 甚至認為雕塑家必須扮演猶如建築師的角色，設置其雕塑的環境則可比擬為一件「巨型雕塑」（une gigantesque sculpture）[7]。在駁二碼頭開展的「無限上鋼」，即嘗試探究大型雕塑的「建築性」，挖掘雕塑「形構空間」的潛力。不僅企求與港岸地景相映、與現代都會以及自然地理對話，更探尋參與港都新貌的塑造、參與城市之「空間實踐」的可能。

另外，在材料的問題方面，充足無虞的材料供應，無疑為藝術家發想並完成大型雕塑的重要關鍵。本屆鋼雕藝術節的創作材料，續由東和鋼鐵公司提供。以每位藝術家 20 噸，總計達 120 噸的廢鋼鐵，超越一般雕塑創作營的大量而充裕的材料[8]，催發並支援藝術家的大型創作。

藝術家們從東和鋼鐵廠的廢材儲存區，挑選創作所需。來自世界各地、等待被重新融熔提煉為鋼材的大量廢鋼鐵，涵蓋現代建築的鋼鐵構件或日常生活的金屬器物等等，經拆卸解構、軋壓而扭曲變形。各式的鋼鐵物件與碎片，有機、多變與混雜的樣態，正對應並消解了創作營的「限材」創作中單項、一致而同質的材料框架。

廢棄鋼鐵物件的豐富符號蘊意，刺激自由異想；種種碎片的紛繁形貌，啟發造型的開放。殊異多樣的廢鋼鐵，就猶如解放想像的觸媒，成為藝術家創作發想的重要根源。這種隨選廢材、現地創作的方

式，因而不僅和「拾得物」（Found object）的概念也特別和與之相關的「集合藝術」（assemblage）的造型邏輯，有所連結。

超現實主義的「拾得物」，是一種召喚歷史的形式，活化高度承載「過去」的事物為「現在」服務；並且，也是一種對於理性主義的質疑，將藝術創作的選材，開放給偶然和機遇，以解放理性意識的禁制，擁抱各種可能的意外與驚奇。面對廢鋼鐵材料，「無限上鋼」創作營既立基於「拾得物」的「發現」或說「偶然」美學，削減既定制約，促發變動、碰觸未知。

源出「拼貼」（collage）傳統的「集合藝術」，則主要是以物件（尤其是「拾得物」）的群集、堆積與組合來創作。同樣的，「集合藝術」亦對於與素材之間足以激發想像的偶然機遇，有所著墨，仰賴感性直覺更甚於理性研究與縝密思慮。在實踐上，「集合藝術」類近即興組合可得的既有材料，以進行探索與實驗之「隨創」作為（bricolage）。Allan Kaprow 在他 1966 年的《集合、環境和偶發藝術》中，既以一種「隨創」的拼貼雕塑的概念，來描述「集合藝術」。

焊接組構廢鋼鐵的雕塑，類屬於廣泛的「廢棄物雕塑」，一般也歸為是一種「集合藝術」的表現。「無限上鋼」創作營，大體上也可説是以「集合藝術」手法為實踐的基礎方法論，其中機動與彈性的「隨創」精神，亦在創作營的各式藝術探索過程中有不同程度與階段性的體現，尤其是鋼鐵雕塑直接構作的特性，使得藝術家的想法與實作得以亦步亦趨，利於「隨創」的發展。然而，這卻並非是創作營充分的美學框架。

事實上，「偶然隨機」和「規劃安排」在創作營中有著微妙的對話與折衝調配。在不同藝術家的雕塑中，其間的運作並且大有差別。如果説 Polissky 和尚曉風，乃是依材料、隨感受來發想創作，梁任宏的動態雕塑或是 Cordero 簡潔的幾何造型，則較多是預設計畫的落實執行。然而，不論何者，在「無限上鋼」所訴求的大型公共雕塑的創作過程中，牽涉到的都並非是全然的隨性拼組與任意堆砌，而更是根據相互關係 —— 不論是物理造型或抽象意義上的 —— 來進行的組織與構成。這種以某種「有機性」的邏輯來整合碎片、組構敘事的創作，正折射出新世紀「集合藝術」及其時代意義的演化。

二十世紀經 William Seitz 於 1961 年明確指認的「集合藝術」中，隨創性的物件群集與堆砌，反映大量生產與消費的資本主義社會，也觀照了資訊宛如瀑布宣洩一般地洶湧而至的時代。二十一世紀的當代雕塑中，「集合藝術」成為相當普遍的表現手法，Laura Hoptman 以「趨近碎片的 21 世紀」（Going to Pieces in the 21st Century）為題的專文裡，甚至論斷這是新世紀最有趣的當代雕塑中幾乎都共享的美學特質之一。然而，如果說作為某種「時代轉喻」的集合藝術表現，在這新世紀之初，同樣也回應了各式資訊更是爆量龐雜的新時代的話，它與上一世紀之別，卻也值得進一步區辨。Hoptman 揭示了其中一項關鍵差異：新世紀以來的「集合藝術」表現中，種種元素往往並非隨機排列，相反地，常是仰賴其意義而微妙組構，以其敘事直接連結，一如在各式串流媒體發達、資訊擴增得如無邊無際之大海汪洋的新世紀中必要的生存法則，亦即巧妙的選擇與機智的組織[9]。

「無限上鋼」創作營中將各式廢鋼鐵以新秩序切割重構或直接組合、建立聯繫、進而賦予意義的創作過程，體現一種選用紛雜碎片以構成具意義的形式、組織成一個完整敘事的作為，微妙呼應了饒富時代特質的新集合藝術美學。然而，創作營的藝術家們雖然「趨近碎片」，卻並未一致地停留於碎片。完全消融廢鐵件的原初面貌與符號形式、翻新打造「一體化」造型的「化零為整」美學，在此也見進一步的積極實踐，而其「製造」（making）更甚於是單純的「群集」、「堆積」的表現，根本超越了一般廢鋼鐵雕塑的「集合藝術」範式。

陌生之眼：
從舊物質中翻轉出的新視野

作為藝術媒介的物質材料並非是個純然的客體，它往往依附於藝術家創造性的感知系統，而演繹出不同的意義與存在。「無限上鋼」創作營的「限材」創作模式，「鋼鐵限定」為不變的先決條件下，這尤其是左右藝術語言創發與新義生產的重要關鍵。與客體對象建立新穎而富創造性的關係，特別是「陌生化」美學的要旨。其核心概念，簡言之，乃是透過將熟悉的客體對象轉化為陌生的方式，破除事物的理所當然或平凡無奇，以激活感知、重新發現、

建構差異的獨特視野。「陌生化」這個於二十世紀初期俄國形式主義文學理論中首見的概念，也可在德國劇作家 Bertolt Brecht 之「史詩劇場」（epic theatre）的「距離化」（distanciation）理論、或是其中的「去自然化」（dénaturation）和「去平庸化」（débanalisation）的論點中，發現迴響。法國哲學家 Gaston Bachelard 視「陌生化」為「想像」的固有作用，在《空間詩學》裡，他說明了「陌生化」的效果：「在它新奇而獨特的活動中，想像讓熟悉的事物化為陌生，以一個詩意的細節，在我們面前開啟一個全新的世界」[10]。「無限上鋼」中來自歐亞不同文化背景的藝術家們，正猶如翻轉熟悉與慣常、萌發新穎觀想的一雙雙「陌生之眼」。他們重新看待與思考鋼鐵物質，挖掘殊異的藝術表現可能，或藉以進行造型實驗、物象探索、空間構築，或藉以傳達寓言訊息、揭示對世界的觀察與提問，提供新的感知與體驗，開啟不同的視野。

Cordero 於創作營期間所完成的《天上大誌》，全然改變了我們對於廢鋼鐵的既定印象。猶如某種工業化秩序的還原或復歸一般，鋼鐵廢材轉化為俐落平整、簡約精鍊的抽象幾何。僅餘刻意保留的碎片焊接痕跡、暗褐鏽色，為其原來材料留下註記。Cordero 以幾何形中最為完滿也最富動態的圓形，做為造型基礎。在構成雕塑主體的兩截 C 字型的半圓之間，圓的建構與解構、完整與斷裂、閉闔與開展，彷彿併陳，營造出動態張力以及不穩定平衡。在空間中建立某種結構，為 Cordero 藝術實驗的方

瑞卡多・柯德羅《天上大誌》

向。這種雕塑探索，趨近於建築。藝術家既曾直言自己「猶如以雕塑來創建建築，以雕塑來改造並介入空間」[11]。這個觀念，也將 Cordero 帶到了作品所在空間的思考，並把和觀眾的關係納入考量。《天上大誌》即是如此。與具有固實量體而「佔有」空間的雕塑類型不同的，此作藉「線性」造型，「解放」空間，以在作品 - 場所 - 觀眾之間建立對話。其中的「線性」形式，因此並非為劃定界限，而是相反的，嘗試敞開一個創造交會與互動、乃至引發觀看與發現的美學場域。

與 Cordero 迥然不同的，以舊鋼管為主要材料的前田哲明，展現的是破壞工業生產的標準化幾何形式所發展而來的雕塑語彙。他創作的《無題2015 ——高雄》，以直豎的長條厚鋼板建構核心骨幹後，既不規則地切割大口徑的舊鋼管，裁剪出宛如捲曲破碎的枯葉或紙片的形狀，層層疊疊地組構而成。如果說單元重複，為其中的造型方法，重複的方式，卻沒有公式也無定則。一個個由舊鋼管裁剪而來的碎片單元，既相像又有別。如此具變化的重複，似乎微妙寓示了自然萬物繁衍的有機秩序與存在的樣態。這些重複的單元朝垂直向度發展所構成的「連續體」，既像往上竄升的哥德教堂，亦如高聳的林木，表現生命萌生、成長、發展的意象。

然而，處處的碎片與裂口、斑斑鏽色的粗糙與陳舊，卻也牽引出古代遺址或自然廢墟的聯想。衰滅與蔓生、破敗與崇高，在此交織。探尋藝術溝通和美學體驗新形式的前田哲明，另也在作品的下方，保留了一處開口，邀請觀眾進入，感受穿梭於多層次圓管之間的海風，品味抬頭仰望時所發現的不一樣的天空，也靜心體會自我與作品之間的直接感通。

Polissky 則嘗試挖掘廢鋼鐵物件的「敘事性」，延伸發展其原本的符號訊息與蘊意。在《錨鏈機》中，他直接利用一大綑回收的舊鐵鏈，一圈圈地捆繞在一個大型的工業輪軸上，組成形如某種升降或捲收船舶錨鏈的機械構造。這猶如以考古學的方式重構的《錨鏈機》，立於港口岸邊，像是紀念碑一般地召喚著工業與港灣記憶。錨鏈的一端，並且深沒入海中，強化船舶繫泊的意象，也凸顯此作不論在抽象意義或實際存在上，與它所在的港都碼頭之間的緊密關連。Polissky 不僅立意回應高雄的港都環境與歷史文化，也企圖連結在地生活。在創作營充裕的材料與配備支援下，他創作了第二件作品《聖火》。形制雖然宛如西方古廟宇廢墟中的圓柱，但靈感卻是來自在地常民生活中的各式金屬爐火。燃燒木料而實際點燃之後，自圓柱頂端不斷向夜空噴發的星火，為鋼鐵雕塑加入了新穎元素，也特別見

前田哲明《無題 2015 ——高雄》

尼古拉‧波利斯基《錨鏈機》

尼古拉‧波利斯基《聖火》

尚曉風《海之夢》　　　　　　　　梁任宏《What is 花枝》　　　　　　劉柏村《雲端漫步》

證了從「人間煙火」到「聖火」幾近神話般的奇妙昇華。

懷抱開放的態度，以即興與隨創精神直接面對鋼鐵廢材之多樣可能的尚曉風，於東和鋼鐵廠，發現了拆解自橋樑建築和大型機械的廢鋼鐵組件。在他眼中，這些曾承載極大重力而於回收之際又經巨大力量扭曲變形的材料，傳達了獨特的能量。「這將是我新作品的靈魂」[12]，尚曉風說道。在他所完成的《海之夢》中，豎立於 S 形的基座上、以厚鋼板焊接拼組成的圓盤，宛如飛碟，亦似某種海貝；在其上方，扭曲的 H 鋼樑，向空中延展，有如迎風翻滾擺動的緞帶，圈畫出像是飄遊浮雲的輪廓，也猶似隨浪扭身起舞的某種海中生物。在具像的暗示與抽象形式之間，藝術家召喚著海港觀眾的想像與共鳴。來自工業的能量，也在此轉化為富流變動態的造型韻律。

實際地結合鋼鐵的機械秩序與自然的微妙韻律，特別為出生也定居於南臺灣的梁任宏所擅長。以此完成的大型動態藝術，是他最具代表性的創作路線。他這次藉廢鋼鐵所發想的風動雕塑《What is 花枝》，上半部是以光澤銀亮的不鏽鋼打造的喇叭狀四肢，猶如某種百合屬的奇花異卉，隨著港都的海風，轉動搖擺；下半身則為由鏽色緻密的鐵材所

形構的鼓圓大腹，以及着有葉片鞋的四足。整體像是某種多腕或複足的頭足類海底生物，亦或是來自科幻星際的不明物種。鋼鐵的厚重、堅硬、強韌的力量，早先曾讓人與宇宙神秘的暗黑能量相聯想；它高溫難耐、折磨人的提煉情境，也曾被與地獄相喻[13]；廢棄鋼鐵更是與廢墟意象有所連結。然而，梁任宏的《What is 花枝》，卻以自然的風動及諧趣的輕盈，翻轉鋼鐵的沈重、超越廢墟的頹敗。此異想生物，引人莞爾又咀嚼反思。它不僅回應港都的海洋環境與工業背景、連結了自然宇宙與文明世界，其中所迸現的幽默與機智火花，正如藝術家借位的擬人化提問「我可愛嗎？人類！」，調侃地提點出在仿生科技與人類失能、文明進展與自然異化之間拉扯發展的現實世界。

近年同樣專注於鋼鐵雕塑的劉柏村，提出了另一番不同的材料發想與自然關照。在他的創作中，劉柏村不僅探索著鋼鐵的物質特性、象徵意義及其「構築空間」的可能性，也藉此蘊含象徵意義的材料，探討工業化為世界帶來的改變，包括它對自然環境與社會生活的影響。創作營期間完成的《雲端漫步》中，他利用凝結成片狀、外形輪廓不規則的煉鋼爐渣，切割表現高掛於空中的流水行雲；並以厚鋼板裁切出鋪陳於地面的片片雲朵，還有高聳直立、併

比成群的林木身影，來構組觀眾得以踏足漫步其間的詩意「雲端步道」。除了在鋼板上勾勒然後切割的施作手法充滿繪畫特質之外，在完成的作品中，不論是地面的雲朵圖案、高空的浮雲線描、或是修長的樹形剪影，也都清楚顯見藝術家玩味從 2D 變換到 3D 的手法，反轉了大尺寸鋼鐵雕塑的量體感，更創造了一幕「符號化的人工自然」。鋼鐵林木與雲朵所共構的這條古木參天的特殊「雲端步道」，不僅對照了高樓林立的現代都會景觀，也反映自然被符號化乃至扁平化的文明社會現象。

※

「鋼鐵限定」的路線、創作營的模式，為這屆高雄國際鋼雕藝術節「無限上鋼」的前提。「無限上鋼」不僅重探「鋼鐵限定」的意義，以實際的創作解放其中的文化生產與創新能量；也探查創作營的制約、侷限與框架，嘗試推演、挑戰或超越，挖掘可能的意義翻轉與新發展。而其中牽引出的「限」與「無限」的對照與辯證，正得以進一步探索創作營這個在國際間行之有年的藝術實踐型態及其獨特意義，開啟不同層次的思考並增添新範例。

在「無限上鋼」中，鋼鐵不但是「可見」，也「可感」乃至「可述」。這不僅指的是物質材料，更包括它牽引出的場所精神與地方記憶，乃至於對世界的觀察與想像。藝術家們殊異獨特的觀看視角，對於作為藝術語言媒介之鋼鐵物質的重新演繹與詮釋，引介了一個特殊的感知維度，提供跨越既有認知或想像模式的可能，拓展對於物質的看法與理解、對人與物甚而對人與世界之關係的不同感受與領會。從「鋼鐵限定」出發，「無限上鋼」終究試圖擴展的是一個比鋼鐵更寬廣的思考或感知領域。

註釋

1 Thomas McEvilley, Sculpture in the Age of Doubt, New York: Allworth Communications, 1999, p. 295.

2 參見李俊賢，〈發揚刮肉性格，復興拼裝文化：機械總動員開展感言〉以及羅潔尹，〈孔鏽樂園：硬梆梆機械中的軟思考：關於「美術高雄 2007：機械總動員」展覽〉，《美術高雄 2007：機械總動員》，高雄市立美術館，2007，頁 4-5；12-31。

3 Jo Murphy, "How Did Junk Sculpture Lead to the Origin of Art Happenings?" https://suite.io/jo-murphy/4ddw21p（2015.02.25 參閱）

4 筆者曾於談論 2012 高雄國際鋼雕藝術節的專文中，初探創作營「限材」與「限地」創作的意義與表現（《2012 高雄國際鋼雕藝術節》專輯，頁 20-27）。

5 Neal Barab, "Stone Sculpture Symposia," in Sculpture Magazine, Vol. 17, No. 4 (1998). http://www.sculpture.org/documents/scmag98/sympos/sm-sympo.shtml（2014.12.20 參閱）

6 Claes Oldenburg, "Interview", in Art Press, July/August 1988, p.14. 轉引自 Florence de Mèredieu, Histoire Matérielle et Immatérielle de l'Art Moderne & Contemporain, Paris: Larousse, 2011, p. 260.

7 Florence de Mèredieu, op.cit., p. 260-261.

8 以最近舉行的創作營為例：智利於 2015 年 2 月期間所舉辦的為期 10 天的國際雕塑創作營，邀集了 11 位雕塑家，以鋼鐵為媒材者，主辦單位提供的材料為 150 公斤的鐵件；又如於 2015 年 9 月 丹麥亞森斯（Assens）舉辦的國際雕塑創作營，兩週的期程，涵蓋兩位當地藝術家在內共計六位受邀藝術家，利用修船廠的廢棄鋼鐵為材料，不僅背景條件與高雄港都類似，活動時間與藝術家數目也和「無限上鋼」相近，然而，每位參與藝術家可使用的材料上限為一噸，而且藝術家原則上必須能夠在獨立作業的情況下進行創作。

9 Laura Hoptman, "Going to Pieces in the 21st Century", Unmonumental, Phaidon, 2007, p. 132-133.

10 Gaston Bachelard, La Poétique de l'Espace, Paris: Les Presses Universitaires de France, 3e édition, 1961, p.161. http://dx.doi.org/doi:10.1522/030329718（2015.04.20 參閱）

11 源出創作營期間筆者與 Cordero 的對談（未出版）。

12 參見藝術家的創作理念自述。

13 參見 André Ughetto : "Préface", Les Sculpteurs du Métal, 66 Portraits d'Artistes, Paris : Somogy Editions d'Art, 2006, pp.9-13.

"Steel Super": About the 2014 Kaohsiung International Steel & Iron Sculpture Festival

■ Curator: Liu Chun-Lan,
Professor of the Department of Sculpture, National Taiwan University of Arts

The theme of the 7th Kaohsiung International Steel & Iron Sculpture Festival (KISISF) in 2014, "Steel Super", is inspired by the term "Unlimited Supremacy" derived from Marxism-Leninism, which describes the exaggerating interpretation and unduly means in political criticism. "Steel Super", borrowing the ideas but overturning the negative connotation in its original context, illuminates and rethinks the character and attributes of the "steel-and-iron-limited" city festival in Kaohsiung; moreover, it attempts to transcend and expand the scope and vision of the art event in the port city. Riccardo Cordero (Italy), Nikolay Polissky (Russia), Noriaki Maeda (Japan), Shang Xiao-Feng (China),

Liang Jen-hung (Taiwan), and Liu Po-Chun (Taiwan) worked on-site in the Pier-2 Art Center to extend beyond the tie of steel and industry, and re-shape the aesthetic relationship between steel and art, with distinctive perspectives and approaches.

Steel and iron limited: from industrial production to cultural creation and innovation

This year's KISISF again launched as a workshop, a common pattern presumably initiated by the 1959 International Sculpture Symposium organized by Karl Prantl. Prantl invited artists to create and permanently install outdoors large sculptures with local stones at a deserted stone quarry in St. Margarethen in Eastern Austria. Sculptors were invited by certain units or groups to engage in public on-site projects to work with local materials in different communities, mines or bases in a limited time. It has since then become the model for international workshops.

While the model Prantl established is for stone sculpture workshops, an early example of steel and iron workshops are those organized in Ravne, Northern Slovenia, in 1964, as part of the "Forma Vivia" sculpture workshops featuring different media in different locations. The first two workshops inspired by Prantl's model featuring stone and wood were set up in 1961, which was followed, three years later, by the steel and iron workshops

in Ravne, a major city of steel and iron based on the industrial tradition of northern Koroška region, as an attempt to incorporate works using modern materials into the intricate fabric of urban space.

Modeled after Prantl's workshops, or more specifically, the Ravne workshops, "Steel Super" workshop also featured local materials: steel and iron, especially recycled steel and iron. Generally, materials as artistic media have dual attributes: they induce us to gaze on their materiality, and they have meaningful messages and connotations for our readings. In his study of the late modern and postmodern sculptures, the art historian Thomas McEvilley used the term "an iconography of materials" to describe that materials are not only to be looked at, but also to be "read" to reveal its connotations.[1] It is particularly true to KISISF, which is rooted in the local context.

Kaohsiung prospers on steel and iron industry: The first iron factory in Taiwan opened in the city in 1919; steel industry flourished in the post-Pacific-War period, as a large number of sunken ships at the port and old ships in other countries gave rise to ship-breaking industry; steel and iron factories of various sizes have risen and thrived... Steel and iron not only shape its industry, abut also its culture. To today's Kaohsiung, steel and iron are more than industrial materials; they are firmly embedded in its cultural fabric. *Mechanical Art in Kaohsiung* (Kaohsiung Museum of Fine Arts, 2007), drawing on the local industrial context, attempted to capture the straightforwardness and perseverance of the society developed for years, as well as the cultural character of "shred/reassemble" cradled in scrap metal or ship-breaking industries, with works that are intense, grassroots, and so on.[2] In fact, its ship-breaking yards and streets of hardware stores have been attracting artists since the 1970s and 1980s. Scrap metal has been used by artists committed to steel-and-iron sculptures for a long time. That material production in the real world has affected every aspect of aesthetic life fully manifests the concept of "cultural integration". It also reminds one of an opportune analogy made by Richard Stankiewicz, the pioneer of junk sculpture, on the junk art developed by New York sculptors in 1955: It is as natural as the South Pacific Islanders using shells in their creations.[3]

"Steel and iron limited" originated from and represented the close tie between Kaohsiung and steel and iron industry, and extracted from it the fundamental cultural context of the city. And it involves not only steel and iron as materials, but also machines, instruments, and equipments processing the materials, the industrial character of teamwork and collective labor, and in particular the cultural background and city history of scrap metal and ship-breaking industries refracted in the procedures of cutting, dissembling, reassembling, and welding.

If memories have significance here, the call of the "Steel Super" workshop for large sculptures is particularly reminiscent of memorials. But more than requesting static signs pointing to the already deep-seated memories, "Steel Super" highlighted the "contemporizing", recounting, and rewriting of collective industrial memories as individual improvisations were turned into public activities like performance art. In the steel and iron world of the workshop, spatial perceptions grew with temporal memories, which not only evoked and renewed people's memories of Kaohsiung, but also witnessed, and even participated in, its transformation and cultural evolution from industrial to post-industrial periods.

In the age of globalization, "steel and iron limited" is exceptionally radical, when viewed as a means to produce cultural differences. The participation of artists of different nationalities re-interpreted the local cultural context with a specific historical depth on the international level, while introducing differences into the local culture. It generated a reflexive perspective, inquired into the possibilities to update and enrich it, and activated the dynamics of cultural differences. In sum, 'steel and iron limited' did more than responding to the production of industrial materials; more fundamentally, it encouraged cultural creation and innovation -- locally, as well as generally.

Facing the limits and rules: from surpassing the limits to challenging the established rules

Improvising with steel and iron, the 6 artists stayed in Dock 3, Pier-2, for 18 days. Apart from "steel and iron limited", that is, the limit on medium, the "Steel Super" workshop of KISISF also had limits on location and time. However, they functioned to encourage, rather than discourage, breakthroughs. The "Steel Super" workshop had the essential goal to transcend the limits, and further, to challenge the established rules, reality, and aesthetic frameworks, for a new expression of steel and iron sculptures.

The limit on location is inherent with a liberating and transcending force worthy of exploration. That for the "Steel Super" project, the artists of different nationalities had to leave their studios and worked in public at specific locations in the Pier-2 cannot be taken as a mere change of locations. It cannot be likened to Claude Monet's "studio-boat", a boat designated as a movable studio for outdoors sketching. Instead, what the limit on location inaugurated was an art practice going beyond the default settings of the studio. The artists encountered a sweeping change of physical conditions that stimulated a breakaway from habitual expressions and

established premises. The challenge to habits and the normal state triggered reflection, contemplation, and self-excavation, while calling forth reactions to the stimulation and inspiration of the local environment. The works *in situ* that were closely related to the local space or history were different from works made in the studio.[4] The interaction of artists working simultaneously in the workshop is another factor not to be neglected. The exchanges of creative experiences and perspectives of the invited artists forged a collective creativity, fostered new sensitivity and potential, and opened up new possibilities for the limit on location.

To artists, majestic, large-scale, and often unaffordable sculptures are a perfect embodiment of how physical limits can be inverted, as Neal Barab's praised that, "A sculpture symposium is the sculptor's fantasy come true". Experienced in working in foreign countries, the artist even thought that it was why Prantl set up workshops.[5] If large-scale installations have been the primary concern of workshops since its germination, they also offer an opportunity for artists. More than offering the opportunity, "Steel Super" supported the artists to create colossal works as tall as 5 meters, a size exceeding those supported by the former KISISFs. Among the completed works, Shang Xiao-Feng's sculpture has a height of 6.3 meters, and Liu Po-Chun's sculpture is more than 9 meters tall and wide.

Sculptures of so gigantic a scale certainly illustrate the possibilities of working in a limited time. Their realization demanded a lot of work. "Steel Super" assisted the artists on large-scale works with adequate and timely equipments and technical support: cranes, forklift trucks, aerial lift vehicles and other necessary supplies, and notably, 26 assistants and 2 electricians. For the first time, KISISF registered the participation of local cooperators, including Technical Director Tsai Kun-Lin,

Technical Supervisor Cheng Yang-Cheng, and the team led by Su Chien-Yin, in written form. The pseudo-engineering process indicated not only the artists' integrative creativity, but also the "aesthetics of production" combining collective work and intensive labor in large-scale steel and iron sculptures.

Sculptures higher than 5 meters are actually rare in workshops. What enabled "Steel Super" workshop to improvise gigantic sculptures in a limited time was closely related to the nature of steel and iron: they are easy to pack and assemble with industrial techniques such as cutting and welding, and can be worked on directly, rapidly, immediately, and reversibly. The "Steel Super" works had again enacted and explored the features and potentials of steel and iron as an exceptional medium to be applied directly on site.

Aside from displaying the character of steel and iron sculptures in public, the on-site large works also invited their visitors to engage in lively visual and physical interactions. Take Liu Po-Chun's *Roaming Over Clouds* and Noriaki Maeda's *Untitled 2015 -- Kaohsiung* as examples, the visitors could not only circle around, but also walked into them, to feel and experience their openness.

The size of sculptures conditioned by the space in which they situate affects their relationship with the environment, their implications and functions. In 1988, Claes Oldenburg remarked on his colossal public sculptures of magnified everyday objects that, "We infused architectural functions into practical, personal objects, and related them to the location which contained them".[6] As suggested by Florence de Mèredieu's recent discussion of "L'architecture de l'espace", not just Oldenburg, other artists such as Louise Nevelson and Jean Dubuffet had also witnessed how large outdoors sculptures can function to invigorate the relationship between the sculpture and its environment: by means of intervention, contrast, connection,

integration, and even construction. Nevelson even thought that sculptors must play the role of architects, and that the environment where the work is installed is "une gigantesque sculpture".[7] "Steel Super" in Pier-2 had attempted to scrutinize the "architectural quality" of large sculptures, and unearth their potential in "constructing a space". The works sought to respond to the port landscape, commence dialogues with the urban space and the natural geography, and further participate in the formation of a new port landscape, as part of the spatial practice of the city.

Meanwhile, an abundant supply of materials was certainly a key to artists on large sculptures. Materials for this year's KISISF were again provided by Tung Ho Steel Enterprise Corporation. A total of 120 tons of scrap steel and iron, exceeding those offered by common sculpture workshops[8], was distributed to the 6 artists, each of whom had 20 tons.

The artists chose what they needed from the storage area of Tung Ho Steel Factory. The steel and iron from around the world waiting to be refused and re-welded into building materials, including those from modern architectures and metal objects from everyday life, were twisted and distorted by disassembling and pressing. Objects and fragments of organic, changing, and mingled shapes both echoed and dissolved the workshop's framework of exclusively focusing on a single medium.

The wealth of implications of steel and iron scraps was a stimulant to imagination; the assortment of shapes was an inspiration to figuration. Their heterogeneity was an important catalyst to the artists' creativity. The approach of selecting scrap materials and improvising in situ is relevant to the concept of "found object", and in particular, to the figurative style of assemblage art.

The surrealist found object is a way of summoning history, of enlivening the objects laden with 'the past' in the service of "the present". It is also a doubt about rationalism, which enables chance and coincidence to liberate the constraint of reason for various possibilities and surprises. Drawing on the "aesthetics of discovery", or "aesthetics of chance" of found objects, the "Steel Super" workshop used steel and iron in an attempt to loosen the grip of the established rules, facilitate change, and reach for the unknown.

Assemblage sprung from the tradition of collage creates primarily by assembling, accumulating, and combining objects (especially "found objects"). It also emphasizes the role of chance encounters between the artist and the objects, and relies more on sensitivity and instinct than on rational analysis and deliberation. In practice, assemblage resembles "bricolage" that examines and experiments by joining together available found objects randomly, as described by Allan Kaprow in his 1966 *Assemblage, Environments and Happenings*.

Sculptures welded from steel and iron scraps can be categorized as "junk sculpture", which is typically seen as a kind of assemblage. In general, the "Steel Super" workshop took assemblage as its methodology. Its spirit of bricolage stressing mobility and flexibility was perceivable in different degrees at different stages of creation. Improvisation that instantly united ideas and practice further facilitated its evolvement. However, the workshop functioned in a larger aesthetic framework.

In fact, chances and plans had intricate dialogues and negotiation in the workshop, which differed from artist to artist greatly. While Polissky and Shang Xiao-Feng created from how they felt about the materials, Liang Jen-hung's dynamic sculpture and Cordero's simple, geometric sculpture followed predetermined plans. Whichever side they fell on, "Steel Super" workshop's call for large public sculptures was less concerned with utter randomness than with organizing and constituting

to coordinate chance and plan, both in figurative and abstract senses. This kind of "organic" logic to coalesce fragments into narratives projects a new assemblage, with a new aesthetics, for the age.

In the assemblage works of the 20th century identified by Williams Seitz in 1961, objects gathered and piled up to reflect the mass production and consumption of the capitalist society, and to observe the age characterized by torrents of information. In sculptures of the 21st century, assemblage has becomes a common way of expression. Laura Hoptman even argued, in her essay titled "Going to Pieces in the 21st Century", that this is an aesthetic feature shared by almost every of the most interesting contemporary sculptures of the day. However, if, as a kind of metaphor of the 21st century, assemblage responds to the even larger explosion of information, it has something different from the assemblage of the previous century. Hoptman showed one of the key differences: the assemblage works of the new century do not randomly deploy dissimilar elements; instead, the elements are directly connected to each other by narratives in a meaningful, subtle way. They are ingeniously selected and wisely organized, so to speak, to simulate drops seeking to survive in a boundless ocean of information in an age dominated by streaming media[9].

"Steel Super" cut, re-constituted, or directly combined scrap metals in a new order, and re-associated and infused meanings into them. The process of constructing fragments into a meaningful whole, a complete narrative, reminds one of the aesthetics of the new assemblage of the age. "Going to pieces" as they were, the artists did not cling to the fragments. The dissolution of the original face and signs of the scrap metals, the aesthetics of 'piecing together' the fragments into a new unity, implies a further, active practice. More than merely "gathering" and "piling up", the process of "making" has transcended the practice of assemblage essential to common junk sculptures.

Strangers' Eyes: A New Vision Projected by Old Objects

Materials used as an art medium are not purely objects. They often develop different meanings and lives in the perceptive system of the artists. The premise of "steel and iron limited" of the "Steel Super" workshop was the key to create and re-define a new language of art. A new and creative relationship with the object is the aesthetic core of "defamiliarization", a concept which, in a word, proposes to turn a familiar object into something un-familiar, to dissociate it with banality, to place it in a different, unique vision for new perceptions and discoveries. The concept first seen in the Russian formalist literary criticism is also found in the Ger-man playwright Bertolt Brecht's concept of "distan-tiation", or "denaturatoin" and "debanalisation", as he discussed epic theatre. The French philosopher Gaston Bachelard regarded "defamiliarization" as an essential function of imagination, as he ex-plained in *The Poetics of Space*", "... the imagina-tion, by virtue of its freshness and its own peculiar activity, can make what is familiar into what is strange... the imagination confronts us with a new world".[10] With "strangers' eyes", "Steel Super" art-ists from European or Asian cultural backgrounds inverted the familiar and the common, and de-vised new perspectives. They reconsidered and rethought the materials of steel and iron, and excavated heterogeneous artistic possibilities, by means of which they experimented with figuration, surveyed phenomena, and constructed spaces, or they conveyed metaphors, observed and raised questions about the world, submitted new percep-tions and experiences, and provided different vi-sions.

Riccardo Cordero's *Grande segno nel cielo, 2014* had thoroughly changed our impressions of

scrap metals. Steel and iron scraps were trans-formed into a smooth, succinct, and refined geo-metric shape, as if the industrial order was restored or reestablished. The traces of welding and rusts were intentionally retained to register their sources. Cordero took circle, the most fulfilling and dynamic geometric shape, as his motif. The two C-shapes or semi-circles constructed and deconstructed, in-tegrated into and disrupted, closed and opened up the sculpture, collaborating to produce a dynamic tension and an unstable balance. As part of Cor-dero's experiment on establishing structures in the space, it explored the space like architecture. As the artist had stated, it is as if he was "establishing architecture, and reshaping and intervening in the space with sculptures".[11] It brought Cordero to think

Liang, Jen-Hung "What is a Cuttlefish?"

about the space where the work was installed, and take its relationship with the visitors into consideration. What distinguishes *Grande segno nel cielo, 2014* from other sculptures that substantially "occupy" the space is that, the work of lines "liberated" the space to set up a dialogue between the sculpture, the location and the visitors. Rather than demarcating, its "lines" served to reveal an aesthetic field that creates encounters, interactions, observations, and discoveries.

By contrast, Noriaki Maeda used old steel tubes to forge a language destroying the standard geometric form of industrial production. In *Untitled 2015 — Kaohsiung* structured by long, vertical, thick steel, old and wide tubes were irregularly cut into layered shapes of curled and broken leaves or pieces of paper. If repetition was its method, it had no formula or rule. The fragments of old tubes were both similar and dissimilar to each other. The variant repetition seemed to elaborately embody the organic order and existence of all living things,

as the "continuum" of repetitive, vertical elements expressed the germination, growth, and development of life, while resembling a towering Gothic church. However, fragments and rifts, the crude and old rusts, also reminded one of ancient ruins or natural relics, in which the animate and the inanimate, the ruined and the sublime interweaved. The artist seeking new ways to communicate and experience also left an opening at the bottom of the work, which invited the visitors to enter and feel the sea wind flowing through the layered tubes, look up to find a different sky, and commune with the work in tranquility.

Nikolay Polissky attempted to formulate a "narrative" of scrap steel and iron by developing and deepening their inherent messages and implications. Braadspil used a huge load of recycled chain cables to bundle a large capstan to form something like a windlass for raising or lowering the anchor. The windlass re-formed in an archaeological way was then set up on the harbor as a monument

Riccardo Cordero   "Grande segno nel cielo, 2014"

Nikolay Polissky "Braadspil & Sacred Fire"

evoking the industrial memories. That one end of the chain went into the ocean suggesting a harbored boat pinpointed the connection between the work and the harbor where it was located, both conceptually and physically. Polissky intended to respond not only to the environment, history, and culture of the port city, but also to the local life. Amply supplied by the workshops, he made the other work "Sacred Fire". Shaped like a column of the ancient Western temples, it was nevertheless inspired by stove fires commonly seen in the local life. The fire of burned woods sparked on top of the column in the night sky added a new sensation to the metal sculpture, while witnessing the mythical, fabulous sublimation of secular fire into sacred fire.

Shang Xiao-Feng, with an open mind and a spirit of bricolage, found metal fragments removed from bridges and large machines in Tung Ho Steel Enterprise Corporation. In his eyes, these materials heavily pressured and distorted as a constituent of a machine and in the process of recycling were remarkably powerful. "This will be the spirit of my new work".[12] Shang said, before *Dreams of Ocean* was realized. Erected on a S-shaped podium, *Dreams of Ocean* welded from thick steel looked like a flying saucer or a sea shell, with twisted H beams stretching upward like ribbons in the wind, clouds floating in the sky, or some kind of sea creatures dancing in the waves. The figurative and the abstract interacted to animate the visitors' imagination and resonances. Industrial energy was transpired from fluid, volatile contours.

Born and settled in the southern Taiwan, Liang Jen-hung is proficient in combining the mechanic order of metal and the graceful melody of nature, as presented by his large dynamic sculptures. The upper part of the kinetic wind sculpture *What is a Cuttlefish?* are four horns made of shiny and silver stainless steel, which sway and twirl in the sea wind, like some kind of rare species of lilies.

Noriaki Maeda "Untitled 2015 – Kaohsiung"

Shang, Xiao-Feng "Dreams of Ocean"

It lower part is a bulging belly with delicate rusts and four feet in leafy shoes. As a whole, it looked like a cephalopod with multiple tentacles in the deep ocean or an unknown object from the sci-fi galaxy. The thick, hard, and tough character of steel and iron was once associated with the dark energy of the mysterious cosmos, the intolerably high temperature in steelmaking is compared to that of purgatory,[13] and scrap metals recalls of ruins and relics. Liang Jen-hung's *What is a Cuttlefish?*, however, had inverted the images of heaviness and dilapidation by its kinetic design and lightheartedness. This fantasy creature was both humorous and inspiring. It harked back to the city's oceanic environment and industrial background, connected human civilization to the universe, and the humor and wit burst forth from the question "Am I cute, humans?" posed by the creature jokingly pointed out our reality torn between biomimicry and human disability, civilization and alienation from nature.

Focusing on steel and iron sculpture in recent years, Liu Po-Chun has a different approach to materials and the theme of nature. His work inspects the material quality, symbols, and possibilities of constructing spaces of steel and iron, and analyzes what changes industrialization has brought to the world, including its impacts on the natural environment and our social life. In *Roaming over Clouds* made in the workshop, a poetic "trail in clouds" for wandering visitors was made from thick steel plates cut into clouds on the ground and soaring trees in rows, while irregular sheets of steel slag were cut into clouds in the sky. Aside from the painterly process of outlining and cutting, the contours of the clouds on the ground and in the sky, and the silhouette of the slender and tall trees, exemplified how the artist applied the 2D concept in a 3D project to downsize the volume of the large metal sculpture to signify a landscape of "artificial nature". The "trail in clouds" composed of domineering steel woods and clouds paralleled the modern urban landscape

Liang, Jen-Hung "What is a Cuttlefish?"

Liu, Po-Chun "Roaming over Clouds"

of high-rises, and addressed the social phenomenon of a signified, and even flattened nature.

※

The 2014 KISISF titled "Steel Super", premised by the "steel and iron limited" condition and the workshop, had not only re-defined the condition, liberating its cultural energy and creativity through art-making, but also sought to expand, challenge, or transcend the other conditions, limits, and frameworks of the workshop, and find out possible inversions and new progress. The contrast and dialectics of "limit" and "de-limit" have casted new light on the unique implications of the workshop as an established artistic practice, exhibited a new thinking, and rendered new examples.

In "Steel Super", steel and iron were more than visible; they were also perceivable and enunciable. This involves not only the materials, but also the genius loci and place memories, and further the artists' observations and imaginings of the world. Their different perspectives introduced special perceptual dimensions to the representation and re-interpretation of steel and iron as an artistic medium. They offered the possibility to go beyond the familiar perceptive or imaginary experiences, refresh our opinion and understanding of materials, and bring forth diverse feelings and perceptions of the relationship between humans and things, and even humans and the world. Taking "steel and iron limited" as the starting point, "Steel Super" finally expected to broaden our thinking or perceptive experiences of steel and iron.

Note

1 Thomas McEvilley, *Sculpture in the Age of Doubt,* New York: Allworth Communications, 1999, p. 295.

2. See LI Chun-hsien, "Reviving the Culture of Shredding and Reassembling: *Mechanical Art in Kaohsiung* Opening Speech", and Lo Chieh-yin, "The Playground of Metals: Soft Thinking in Hard Machines: About the 2007 *Mechanical Art in Kaohsiung*", *Art of Kaohsiung 2007: Mechanic Art in Kaohsiung, Kaohsiung Museum of Arts,* 2007, p. 4-5, 12-31.

3 Jo Murphy, "How Did Junk Sculpture Lead to the Origin of Art Happenings?" https://suite.io/jo-murphy/4ddw21p. (Retrieved Feb. 25, 2015.)

4. In an essay on the 2012 KISISF, I have discussed the meanings and expressions of the limits on medium and location of the workshop. See *2012 Kaohsiung International Steel & Iron Sculpture Festival,* p. 20-27.

5 Neal Barab, "Stone Sculpture Symposia," in *Sculpture Magazine,* Vol. 17, No. 4 (1998). http://www.sculpture.org/documents/scmag98/sympos/sm-sympo.shtml. (Retrieved Dec. 20, 2014.)

6 Claes Oldenburg, "Interview", in *Art Press,* July/August 1988, p.14. From Florence de Mèredieu, *Histoire Matérielle et Immatérielle de l'Art Moderne & Contemporain,* Paris: Larousse, 2011, p. 260.

7 Florence de Mèredieu, *op.cit.,* p. 260-261.

8 Take recent workshops for example: A ten-day international sculpture workshop in Chile held in February, 2015, invited 11 sculptors, of whom those working on steel and iron were provided with 150s kilograms of iron materials. Another two-week international sculpture workshop held in Assens, Denmark, in September, 2015, invited 4 foreign artists and 2 local artists to work on scrap steel and iron from a shipyard. The city's being a port city is similar to Kaohsiung, and the workshop's duration and number of artists were also similar to those of "Steel Super". However, its artists were offered no more than 1 ton of metal, and they had to work independently.

9 Laura Hoptman, "Going to Pieces in the 21st Century", *Unmonumental,* Phaidon, 2007, p. 132-133.

10 Gaston Bachelard, *La Poétique de l'Espace,* Paris: Les Presses Universitaires de France, 3e édition, 1961, p. 161. http://dx.doi.org/doi:10.1522/030329718 (Retrieved Apr. 20, 2015)

11 Excerpted from a conversation between Cordero and I during workshop session.

12 See artist statements.

13 See André Ughetto, "Préface", Les Sculpteurs du Métal, 66 Portraits d'Artistes, Paris: Somogy Editions d'Art, 2006, p. 9-13.

鋼鐵之城的藝術之花
—— 從地方文化產業的角度論高雄鋼雕藝術節

文／蕭瓊瑞（國立成功大學歷史系所教授）

台灣雕塑藝術的發展，和地方文化產業的密切關係，在 1990 年代之後，是極為顯著的一個現象。1992 年，花蓮文化中心以其作為大理石產地的地理背景，開始廣收石雕作品，為未來的石雕藝術館進行預備性的工作；1995 年，首辦花蓮國際石雕戶外創作公開賽，成為首屆花蓮國際石雕藝術節。同年（1995），位在苗栗三義的木雕博物館正式開館，成為三義地區木雕產業最具指標性的展示館兼發動機；1997 年，裕隆汽車在廠辦合一於三義後，基於發揚地區文化產業和企業回饋地方的考量，也將 1992 年以來持續舉辦的「裕隆藝文季」，正式定調為「裕隆木雕金質獎」；2003 年起，三義木雕館則持續辦理三義國際木雕藝術節迄今。至於位在台北縣（今新北市）的鶯歌，早在 1988 年，即倡議籌建陶瓷博物館，歷經 12 年努力，在 2000 年，鶯歌陶瓷博物館正式開館，許多深具雕塑性的現代陶瓷作品，亦構成台灣現代雕塑的一個重要面向。

位在南台灣的高雄，早在日據時期，便以工業城市而知名；戰後，更以拆船工業聞名於世。1980 年初，知名藝術家陳庭詩（1916-2002）便展開一系列以高雄拆船業廢材為媒材的鐵雕創作，展現他極具魅力與詩情，又富幽默氣質的傑出創作成果。

1980 年，正是台灣北部藝術家，尤其是一群美術系年輕學子，以水彩為媒材，採照相寫實手法描繪農村景致、標舉鄉土運動正達高峰的時刻；而相同的時刻，一群高雄的畫家，尤其是以現代畫學會為主要成員的藝術家，則正以城市、工業文明為題材，形塑南台灣殊異的文明景觀與現代氣息。

1994 年 6 月，高雄市立美術館開館，如何發掘及建立具有高雄特色的藝術創作，更成為館方和在地藝術家共同努力的目標，2001 年推出的首屆「高雄國際貨櫃藝術節」，正是此一思維下的具體產物；工業的高雄、黑手的高雄、鋼鐵的高雄，也成為在地藝術家自我標舉、自我認同的美學標誌。

貨櫃，做為工業高雄進出口貿易結構下最突顯的語彙，既是城市景觀巨大的視覺元素，也提供了藝術家創作的挑戰。高雄貨櫃藝術節的舉辦，雖非世界首例，但也屬極先進的作為；同為港口城市的丹麥哥本哈根，1996 年獲選為「歐洲文化之都」，為回應這項歐盟國家的城市文化行銷活動，哥本哈根的策展人和藝術家首次以貨櫃作為藝術的載體，舉辦了「貨櫃 96 ——藝術跨洋」（Container 96 -- Art Across Oceans）藝術節；這個跨國性的藝術活動，主辦單位一共寄發了兩百個 20 呎大的船運貨櫃，邀

請遍及全球五大洲九大區域、共計 96 個海洋城市的藝術家，分別在各自居住的地區完成貨櫃創作後，經由海上的長途轉運，最後集中到哥本哈根的港區展出，依九個區域分別設置，再以鷹架相互銜接。在海邊偌大的展場裡，一只只貨櫃被刻意塗成白色，連地面也是鋪滿白色碎石子，整體呈現出北歐城市特有的理性與潔淨氛圍。台灣受邀的藝術家是侯俊明，提出的作品是《Say Yes, My Boy》，見證了這個世界首創的貨櫃藝術節。

2001 年的高雄貨櫃藝術節，在哥本哈根「貨櫃 96──藝術跨洋」的五年後辦理，且以「貨櫃的第 101 種想法」、「後文明」、「童遊貨櫃」、「永續之城」等主題，分年持續辦理；2007 年，更因陽明海運的居中聯繫，參與了由歐洲海港城市發起的「貨櫃藝術組織」，15 件作品前往義大利熱內亞展出。

就在首屆高雄貨櫃藝術節舉辦後的第二年，2002 年，高雄市政府文化局又推出「高雄鋼雕藝術節」，同樣是以工業為特色、以鋼材為媒材，和貨櫃藝術節形成交互隔年舉辦的模式；但由於手法較為自由，不受「貨櫃」的限制，因此在貨櫃藝術節舉辦四屆一度喊停的情形下，鋼雕藝術節仍能持續舉辦迄今 2014 年，已為第七屆，值得肯定，也值得持續期待。

2014 年的高雄國際鋼雕藝術節，邀請國立臺灣藝術大學雕塑教授劉俊蘭擔任策展人，採創作營的模式，以「無限上鋼」為命題，邀請了國內外六位藝術家，包括：義大利的瑞卡多·柯德羅（Riccardo Cordero）、俄羅斯的尼古拉·波利斯基（Nikolay Polissky）、日本的前田哲明、中國大陸的尚曉風，和台灣的梁任宏、劉柏村等人，企圖「藉其不同的觀點、殊異的藝術表現，再度擴展與鋼鐵之間超越工業的聯繫、重新刻寫與鋼鐵的新美學關係。」（策展人語）

「無限上鋼」邀請的六位藝術家，都是已經具有一定知名度的藝術工作者，擁有個人鮮明的風格與豐富的創作經驗，尤其在「鋼鐵」的工業媒材上，更具備熟稔的技巧與想像。此次主辦單位提供的鋼材，是由長期贊助國家藝術文化基金會「藝企合作」的東和鋼鐵企業提供，均為回收的廢鋼鐵，一如 1980 年代陳庭詩以拆船業廢棄的鋼鐵零件為媒材；但不同的是，在策展人期望以「巨型」（超過 5 公尺）來呼應整個展區空間特性的訴求下，現場配備了各式的機具，如：吊車、堆高機、高空作業車與各式必要工具等；此外，又有人數高達 26 位的技術人員擔任助手，以及兩位專業的配電人員，成為歷來大型文化活動中，被正式列名紀錄的「協力藝術家」，也呼應了高雄此一工業之城特有的「黑手藝術家」與「勞動美學」本質。

「巨型尺度」既是策展人針對高雄此一工業之城的空間特色所提出的策展構想，也是針對鋼鐵此一「能焊」、「能接」的媒材特性所發展出來的訴求；因此，在藝術家的邀請上，自然也考量他們曾經有過的類似經驗與成果。

義大利的瑞卡多‧柯德羅，除曾任教美術學院，也兩度受邀在威尼斯雙年展中舉辦個展，早期的作品以結合碎形的有機型態和規則的幾何造型為主；近年則發展出長條方柱彎曲成型的立體式結構，既具理性秩序，又富層次韻律。此次完成的《天上大誌》，在兩截 C 字型的半圓之間，提供了作品空間與觀眾的對話關係，兩個半圓的若合若離，既是圓形的建構與解構，也是動態張力的來源。

俄羅斯的尼古拉‧波利斯基，也是擅長利用巨型雕塑介入戶外空間的知名藝術家；他以模仿、變造知名建築形式作為創作手段而知名，在人工與自然／巨大與渺小間，提供觀眾一次的震撼與感動。此次完成的《錨鏈機》，以回收的大綑鐵鏈，捆繞在一個巨型的工業軸輪上，然後高高立起，猶如一個巨型的紀念碑，錨鏈的一端則垂入海中，形成船舶的意象，也突顯了駁二特區原本作為接駁碼頭的歷史記憶。另一件《聖火》，則以象徵性的手法，再現高雄當地居民宗教金爐或烤食爐火，乃至焚燒木頭時的經驗，深具宗教的儀式性。

來自日本東京的前田哲明，曾旅居英倫多年，獲 2001 年日本當代雕塑雙年展首獎等大獎，也是一位經常以鋼鐵作為創作媒材的知名藝術家，作品講究表面鏽色的處理，粗質卻富歷史感。此次完成的《無題 2015──高雄》一作，仍是著重在鋼材表面的處理，他說：「雖然使用的是廢鋼材，我仍是以在空間中畫素描的感覺來進行創作。」為了讓觀者能更接近體驗，他特別將作品中的一個面大幅度的敞開，誘導觀眾進入，然後站在作品中心，抬頭仰望，看見天空的色彩、感受到風吹過的氛圍，整體造型就像是一雙膜拜的手。

中國大陸的尚曉風，應是此次參展藝術家中年紀較輕的一位，畢業於北京中央美院後，也曾赴澳洲遊學多年。他的作品《海之夢》，是選擇較厚的鋼材，以三個造型元素組成：基座的 S 型，與地面穩定接觸，又有蠕動的感覺；中間是完整的圓形，像個立起來的飛盤，又像某種圓形的海貝，也有滾動的感覺；最上面是部分扭曲的 H 鋼，飛向空中，像雲又像海洋生物。在形象與抽象之間，提供觀眾想像的空間。

台灣的劉柏村，是這幾年相當活躍的藝術家，國立台灣藝專（今國立臺灣藝術大學）畢業後，赴巴黎高等美術學院進修，完成專業養成教育。早年創作媒材多元，且具空間裝置特性；近年則專注鋼雕，曾任東和鋼鐵的駐廠藝術家，對鋼雕創作具有豐富的經驗。此次完成的《雲端漫步》，維持他線形結構的特色，以雲朵及樹形為基本元素。空懸的線描浮雲，是切割自片狀的鋼爐爐渣，地面的雲朵及樹形，則以原鋼板裁切而成。「雲端漫步」一語雙關，既是自然的符號化，也是科技文明的扁平化。

最後一位梁任宏，是道地的高雄在地藝術家，長期以來，以風動、機動雕塑為特色。此次完成的《What is 花枝》，也是一件風動雕塑，上半部以不鏽鋼打造，喇叭狀的造型，既像百合屬的花卉、又像軟體科的海洋生物；下半部鼓圓的大腹及四足，則以鏽色的鐵材形構。「花枝」一詞，本來就有「花」與台語「魷魚」的諧語，從名稱到造形，都充分顯現了高雄土味的霸氣與細膩，既洋又土、既俗又雅。

「無限上鋼」，是策展人劉俊蘭教授以借自馬列主義政治名詞中的語言「無限上綱」，以「鋼」代「綱」，翻轉了政治批判的負面意涵，賦予高雄鋼雕無限寬廣的可能詮釋，為這個原本來自地方文化產業的藝術節慶，提供了「超越」與「擴展」的創作挑戰與視野；既為這個鋼鐵之城，在 2014 年，催生了最奇異、美麗的藝術之花，也為未來高雄鋼雕藝術節的可能發展，激化了更多的可能與可行，應是一次成功的策展。

The Art Flower from the City of Steel and Iron:
On the Kaohsiung International Steel and Iron Sculpture Festival From the Perspective of Regional Cultural Industry

■ Hsiao Chiung-Jui
Professor of the Department of History, National Cheng Kung University

How closely the development of sculpture in Taiwan is related to the local cultural industry has been a dominant concern since the 1990s. In 1992, the Hualien County Cultural Center began to collect stone sculptures using local materials in preparation for the opening of Stone Sculptural Museum. The first Hualien International Stone Sculpture Outdoors Competition was launched in 1995, and was later recognized as the first Hualian International Stone Sculpture Festival. In the same year, Sanyi Wood Sculpture Museum opened as the representative exhibition hall and cultural base for the local wood carving industry. In 1997, Yulon Motors moved its office and factory in Sanyi, and reorganized the Yulon Cultural Festival initiated in 1992 into the Yulon Wood Sculpture Golden Awards to support and promote the local cultural industry. In 2003, Sanyi International Woodcarving Art Festival was held by the Sanyi Wood Sculpture Museum. As to Yingge in the Taipei County (now New Taipei City), it had planned to open Yingge Ceramics Museum as early as 1988, and realized it twelve years later, as the museum opened to the public in 2000. The modern ceramic works with sculptural attributes have become one of the most important aspects of modern sculpture in Taiwan.

Kaohsiung in the Southern Taiwan has been known as an industrial city since the Japanese Occupation, and gained international fame with its ship breaking industry in the postwar period. In the early 1980, the esteemed artist Chen Ting-Shih made a series of iron sculptures with the scrap materials from the ship breaking yards in Kaohsiung. They are excellent examples of his poetic charm and sense of humor.

1980 also witnessed the photorealist watercolor portrayals of the countryside made by the artists from the Northern Taiwan, especially the academically trained young artists, and the full swing of the Nativist Movement. Meanwhile, a group of Kaohsiung painters, mainly the members of the Modern Art Association, began to depict the cultural landscapes and modern atmosphere of the Southern Taiwan with subjects of the city and the industrial civilization.

In June, 1994, Kaohsiung Museum of Fine Arts opened to the public. Its and the local artists' objective was to excavate and support works embodying the characteristics of the city, and one of the concrete results is the first Kaohsiung International Container Arts Festival in 2001. Heavy industry, mechanics, steel and iron that typified Kaohsiung were distilled into the aesthetic expressions of local artists looking for a personal style and cultural identity.

The container as one of the seminal images of the industrial city standing out in its landscape poses challenges to artists. Kaohsiung International Container Art Festival, albeit not the first one, was a remarkably new idea. Copenhagen, another port city in Denmark, was elected as "European Capital of Culture" in 1996. In response to this programme of city marketing and cultural promotion organized by the European Union, the international art project "Container 96 - Art Across Oceans" sent 200 20-foot containers across 9 seas and 5 continents to the artists from 96 seaports, who were commissioned to create an installation in the container and return the containers across the oceans to Copen-hagen. Laid out in 9 sections connected by scaffolds, the containers intentionally painted in white were exhibited on the white gravel in the harbor. The color suggested reason and cleanness of the Scandinavian city. Also invited was the Taiwanese artist Hou Chun-ming, whose "Say Yes, My Boy" witnessed the very first container festival in the world.

The themes of the Kaohsiung International Container Arts Festival, whose fist edition was held 5 years after "Container 96 - Art Across Oceans" in Copenhagen, were "The 101st Way to the Container", "Post-civilization", "GBox: Containers of Children's Memories", and "Sustainable Cosmopolis". In 2007, it took part in Container Art through the Yang Ming Marine Transport Corp., and exhibited 15 containers in Genoa, Italy.

Following the first container arts festival, the Bureau of Cultural Affairs, Kaohsiung City Government, organized the Kaohsiung International Steel and Iron Sculpture Festival (KISISF), another festival addressing the industrial role of steel and iron, in 2002. The two biennial events had since then been staged by turns, until the container arts festival stopped for a period of time after 4 editions. With fewer limits on techniques and physical space, the KISISF entered into its 7th edition in 2014 as a highly acknowledged and expected event.

The 2014 KISISF was curated by Liu Chun-Lan, Professor of the Department of Sculpture, National Taiwan University of Arts. Taking the form of a workshop, it invited 6 foreign and Taiwanese artists, including Riccardo Cordero (Italy), Nikolay Polissky (Russia), Noriaki Maeda (Japan), Shang Xiao-Feng (China), Liang Jen-Hung (Taiwan), and Liu Po-Chun (Taiwan), to respond to the theme "Steel Super". Its goal was to "to extend beyond the tie of steel and industry, and re-shape the aesthetic relationship between steel and art, with distinctive perspectives and approaches" (Liu Chun-Lan).

The 6 artists invited by "Steel Super" are established artists with distinct styles and rich experiences, and are particularly accomplished in transforming steel from industrial materials into an artistic medium. The steel was provided by Tung Ho Steel Enterprise COR., a long-time sponsor of the "art & business cooperation" project directed by the National Culture and Arts Foundation. They were all recycled steel, the kind of scrap steel from ships Chen Ting-Shih had used in the 1980s, but the artists were expected to create "gigantic" (taller than 5 meters) sculptures to accommodate to the space. They were provided with equipments such as cranes, forklift trucks, aerial lift vehicles and other necessary supplies, and a total of 26 assisting technicians and 2 electricians. That the technical team was listed as the formal "assisting artists" was not only exceptional in large cultural activities, but also suggestive of the image of the mechanic-artists and the aesthetics of labor specific to the industrial city.

"Large scale" as the curator's idea to respond to the spatial character of Kaohsiung also implied the welding process of steel and iron. The artists were invited for their related experiences and works.

Riccardo Cordero had taught in the Accademia Albertina di Belle Arti di Torino, and was invited to exhibit in la Biennale di Venezia twice. His early works integrated fragmentary, organic shapes into regular geometric forms; the recent works twisted long metal strips into sculptural structures combining rational order and rhythmic depth. Grande segno nel cielo, 2014 attempted a dialogue with the visitors through the dynamics between the association and dissociation, construction and deconstruction of the two C-shapes

Nikolay Polissky is also recognized for intervening in the open landscape with colossal sculptures, for imitating and modifying renowned architectural forms, and shocking and moving the visitors with

the tension between the artificial and the natural. Braadspil used a sizable load of recycled chain cable on a giant capstan, and erected it as a massive monument, with one end of it went into the ocean suggesting the image of a ship, and the historical memories of the Pier-2 as a harbor. Sacred Fire symbolically representing the incense burner, stove fire, or burning wood commonly seen in the local life is a deeply ritualistic work.

Noriaki Maeda from Tokyo had lived in England for many years, and was the recipient of the first prize of the 2001 Contemporary Japanese Sculpture Biennale. As an artist known for using steel and iron, Maeda's skill in cultivating a sense of history from the color and roughness of rusts was evidenced in Untitled 2015 -- Kaohsiung. "Although I used scrap steel, I created it as if I was making a sketch in the space." To invite the visitors to experience it fully, he designed an opening for them to enter and stand looking up at the sky and feeling

the wind. It is shaped like a pair of worshipping hands.

Younger than the other artists, Shang Xiao-Feng was graduated from the Central Academy of Fine Arts, Beijing, and had spent many years studying and working in Australia. "Dreams of Ocean" made of thick steel sheets has three parts: the S-shaped podium suggesting movement which nevertheless firmly seized the ground; the middle circle, another image of movement looked like an standing flying saucer or a round seashell; the upper H-beam, which was twisted into something like clouds or a sea creature that fly upward. It's oscillation between the figurative and the abstract liberated imagination.

Liu Po-Chun is a very active artist in recent years. He was fully trained in École Nationale Supérieure des Beaux-Arts de Paris, after graduated

from the National Academy of Arts (now National Taiwan University of Arts). Making installations with diverse media in the early years, he turned to focus on steel sculptures in recent years, and was an artist-in-residence in Tung Ho Steel Enterprise CRO. "Roaming over Clouds" characterized by his typical linear structure was primarily built on the images of clouds and trees. The outlined clouds floating in the sky were made from sheets of steel slag, while the clouds on the ground and trees were cut from thick steel plates. The title Roaming over Clouds implied both a symbolized nature and a flattened world of technology.

Liang Jen-Hung is an artist based in Kaohsiung known for kinetic sculptures. What is a Cuttlefish? is also a kinetic work, of which the upper horn-shaped part, also resembled lilies or mollusks, was made from stainless steel, and the lower part, a bulging belly with four feet, was made from iron with rusts. The work itself, and "Hua Chih (cuttlefish)" in the title pronounced like "flower" and "cuttlefish", exemplifies the forcefulness and delicacy of the culture of Kaohsiung. It is simultaneously foreign and local, vulgar and graceful.

"Steel Super (Wu Hsien Shang Kang)" was derived from a Chinese term of Marxism-Leninism. The curator Liu Chun-Lan substituted "kang (steel)" for "kang (agenda)", and thereby inversed the negative implication of the political term, presented possibilities for steel and iron sculptures, and provided the art festival rooted in the local culture and industry with challenges and insights to transcend and expand. It gave birth to both the most bizarre yet beautiful flower of art for the city of steel and iron in 2014, and further opportunities and probabilities for the future KISISFs. This achievement alone made it a success.

創作營的聯想：
記 2014 高雄國際鋼雕藝術節「無限上鋼」

文／賴永興（國立臺灣藝術大學雕塑學系副教授）

當我們看待某一個時期或地區的歷史特色時，在藝術這個項目中是令人最期待的項目，有時這些作品特色甚至會超越其他項目，而成為那個時代或地區的象徵，例如文藝復興時期米開朗基羅的大理石雕像、秦始皇陵四週挖出的兵馬俑、北魏的雲岡石窟、復活節島的摩埃巨石像等等，一看到它們總是容易讓我們聯想到那個時代或是地域的種種。雕塑藝術的創作往往是趨使當時最先進的技術來製作，不論是為了政治或宗教上的目的，總是能從這些立體作品反映出屬於這個時代的許多訊息。2012 年筆者參觀「全民大戀鋼」展覽中的作品有著巨大尺寸和氣勢所感動，去年年底再次拜訪「無限上鋼」之後深信，這些鋼鐵作品已經成為高雄市這個時代的歷史證物。

自 1959 年 Karl Prantl 在奧地利的 St. Margarethen 採石場舉辦第一次的跨國創作營「歐洲雕刻家創作營」之後，目前這個創作營模式已經廣被世界

扇形公園上的鄭宏南作品《看！鋼鐵的聲音》

各地所採用。雖然每個創作營的舉辦目的及執行方式都不一致，基本上可以歸納成五個要件，本文從一個創作營經驗者的角度試著加以論述。

一、行政企劃執行是創作營成案最重要的一環，案件確定以及執行和後續等作業能夠全程掌握的

話，那這個創作營的骨架構造就成形了。高雄國際鋼雕藝術節自 2002 年起到這次「無限上鋼」已經連續舉辦了七屆，就一個國際創作營來說，它的規模夠大夠專業、國際藝術家比例適當、老中青世代兼備、材料準備充分、機具齊全、專業助手團隊、藝術家現身說法，專題座談、持續不中斷等等。這個創作營可以說是一個典範，令人不禁要為背後的營運體系喝采。這些作品的水準都非常高，量體也很巨大，很難想像它們都是在短時間的創作營所製作出來，可見只有執行單位、策展人和贊助單位三方面合作無間的狀況下，藝術家才得以發揮全力，創作出最佳作品。

創作營這種移地創作對藝術家而言是一種極限的挑戰，在時間、空間、設備、材料皆有限制的狀況下，所有藝術家都只能在相同條件下創作，彷彿以前寺廟建築的師傅拼場，雙方都會卯足全力，因為拼的不只是面子，還有裡子。筆者曾經在 2011 年與

2011 羅馬尼亞創作營

宋璽德前往羅馬尼亞參加第三十七屆夏季拉札爾創作營，行前與主辦單位多次溝通創作營所需的機具及材料，特別是把宋老師所需的各種電焊機具及鋼料翻成英文傳過去，獲得的回信是 OK 後，放心出發前往，不料到了創作營後，發現所要求的金屬設備及材料都沒有準備，只有一堆大松木，馬夫牽著馬在一旁，咧嘴笑著問：「您想要刻哪一根？我幫您拖過去。」……結果那次不鏽鋼造形藝術家宋璽德創作了一件大木雕作品。

二、創作基地的在地精神與素材的關連。花蓮是石材產地與石材加工城市；林務局本身是主管林業的政府單位，在其轄區內使用它們才有支配權的漂流木辦創作營；重工業城市高雄則舉辦鋼雕創作營。這些都是所在地與素材間有緊密關聯的例子。有這樣的條件為基礎，創作營的成案就比較容易，藝術家也比較容易深入探討在地與材質間的關聯與涵義，進而容易創作出與在地及材質有交集的藝術作品。

1919 年台灣第一座鐵工廠（打狗鐵工所）成立於高雄，開始了高雄發展重工業的命運；1970 年代十大建設更加速了鋼鐵、石化等產業為這個國際港都帶來繁榮，間接也將高雄形塑成一個支撐台灣的重工業城市。在工業起飛的時代，相較於台北首都，高雄的藝文是被忽略的，但是在駁二藝術特區參觀這次創作營現場及漫步在扇型公園的前次創作營作品之間時，筆者深感高雄在藝術文化上並不想成為台北，也不必成為台北，除原有的高雄市立美術館之外，雖也陸續成立了駁二藝術特區、左營眷村文化園區、衛武營藝術文化中心等新的藝文空間，但是觀察與貨櫃藝術節隔年輪辦的國際鋼雕藝術節的特性，可以感受到要追求具有高雄在地精神的藝術這種心意。

三、創作過程與交流是創作營的重頭戲，創作營從開始到結束必須公開於眾人面前是常規，不管藝術家是否樂意和參觀者對話，最起碼透過視覺，觀者可以看到這個藝術家在創作，而藝術家也看到了觀者在看他並開始產生意義。

創作營除了要創作作品、體驗創作過程之外，參加創作營期間，藝術家之間的交流也非常重要，工作之餘互相了解，並確認有無重複的朋友，以建立起自己的人脈網絡。藝術家在創作時往往是孤獨的，但是創作營卻有夥伴的感覺，那是因為共同生活創作，互相協助交流所致，這樣的情況下容易產生革命情感，會遇到許多創作上的好朋友。除了瞭解異國文化，這種友誼甚至會延伸到日後前往其他國家地區參加創作營或進行其他藝術文化活動。臺藝大雕塑系曾經有邀請老師在創作營認識的藝術家 Erőss István 擔任客座教授的案例，可見創作營在國際交流上是有很大的貢獻，不只是自己要被看見，

也要看見別人。筆者在參加日本及歐洲的創作營時，通常都是在晚餐之後輪流介紹自己的創作及國家，以達到相互交流的目的，鋼雕藝術節的藝術家現身說法更是把交流擴展到一般市民，甚至將座談內容轉成文字留下紀錄。另一場座談的題目是「從創作營到藝術節：藝術生產、城市行銷與文化行動」，筆者也參與了這次座談，以報告三義木雕藝術節與薪傳營的現況和其他發表者交換意見。大部分的創作營都是藉由藝術節活動熱絡在地氛圍，其實主軸就是雕塑創作營，對高雄來說也許偏重城市行銷與文化活動，而三義則除前者所提外還兼有藝術生產的特質，並支撐著每年來客超過百萬的觀光產業。

四、創作營主題的命題與目的是讓創作營被看見的策略，簡潔並且切合舉辦精神的命題往往會令整個創作營目標一致，內部容易有共識，宣傳起來也容易。高雄國際鋼雕創作營歷次的命題都令人有這樣的感覺，從這次的「無限上綱」、2012 的「全民大戀鋼」、2010 的「鋼鋼好」、2008 的「金屬光‧城市的溫度」、2006 的「金屬風」、2004 的「飆焊‧跨界」和第一次的「鋼鐵城市‧雕塑希望」等的命題可以看出材質與地域的緊密關係，而從字面上也可以清楚閱讀到要用鋼鐵雕塑形塑高雄的城市意象。兩年一次的鋼鐵雕塑創作營，不停地傳達著屬於高雄的時代訊息。

五、作品完成前後的公開義務與社會責任，創作過程公開的對象除了外來觀眾之外，參加藝術家都是最好的交流基本盤，除了可以相互交心之外，創作技巧、機具應用交流等，對藝術家及觀眾來說受益良多。結束後的作品陳列展示也是創作營的重要步驟，若是事後將作品拿去販售或由私人收藏，這個創作營的立足點就會顯得比較薄弱而不周全，君不見鋼雕藝術創作營的作品設置在駁二特區的各個角落，使整個特區深具藝術特色；花蓮國際石雕營的作品也設置在花蓮市的景點及交通要道，行車經過這些石雕藝術品時總是令人心曠神怡。若是沒將創作營的作品公開，總是讓人覺得遺憾。

國際鋼雕藝術節穩定發展至今，各種正面能量已逐漸顯現，高雄市也慢慢脫離文化沙漠印象，轉變為文化之都；這些參加藝術家將港都的印象帶回自己的國家，也是一種反向的國民外交。期待高雄國際鋼雕藝術節能持續舉辦，為藝術創作挹注更多的能量。

Some Associations of the Workshop:
On "Steel Super", the 2014 Kaohsiung International Steel and Iron Sculpture Festival

■ Lai Yung-Hsing,
Associate Professor of the Department of Sculpture, National Taiwan University of Arts

When looking at the historical characteristics of a period or a place from the perspective of art, sculpture stands out as a special category to me, and sometimes even stands out among the arts as the symbol of the time or place, as in the cases of Michelangelo's marble statues of the Renaissance period, the Terracotta Army around the tomb of Emperor Qin, the Yungang Grottoes of the Northern Wei Dynasty, the Moai of Easter Island, etc. They suggest the time and place in which they were made. Sculptures are often closely related to the technological development and laden with the political and religious messages of their time. I was moved by the large scale and grandeur of the works of "Steel, Love", the 2012 Kaohsiung International Steel and Iron Sculpture Festival (KISISF). After attending "Steel Super" the last December, I believe that steel and iron sculptures have become the historical witness of Kaohsiung in our time.

Since Karl Prantl organized the first Stone Sculptors Workshop in the stone quarry in St. Margarethen, Austria, workshops have become a prevalent form. Although every workshop has different goals and ways of operation, they generally have five elements which I, as a workshop attendee, will try to explicate in the following paragraphs.

1. Management and operation are the most important aspect of a workshop, whose groundwork depends on a perfect command of the whole process. The KISISF has had 7 editions from its inauguration in 2002 to the 2014 "Steel Super". As an international workshop, it is proportionally large and professional, has an appropriate percentage of foreign artists across generations, sufficient materials, equipments, technical support, and assistants, a succession of artist' talks, speeches, and discussions. Its model of management and operation is praiseworthy. The sculptures are so outstanding in quality and large in volume that it is almost unimaginable how they were completed in a limited time. Only when the organizer, the curator, and the sponsors cooperate perfectly that the artists are able to create their best works.

Workshops push the limits of the artists by moving them out of their studios. All of them must work under the same limits of time, space, equipments, and materials, as if they are the temple craftsmen risking their name and career to outmatch each other. In 2011, Sung Hsi-Te and I attended the 37th Lăzarea International Art Camp, Romania. Before we left for Lăzarea, we contacted the organizer several times to ensure that the tools and materials we needed were ready, and even emailed an English list of the welders and steel materials that Sung needed. We received a confirmation email. However, we arrived to find nothing more than a load of pine woods. The groom stood by the horse grinned and asked which trunk we would like to be carried to the camp... Sung as a sculptor of stainless steel ended up making a large wood sculpture.

2. The connection between local culture and local materials. Hualien is the source and manufacturer of stones. Forestry Bureau as the governmental unit managing forestry has organized driftwood sculpture workshops using the woods from its administrative regions. And Kaohsiung, the city of heavy industry, has steel sculpture workshops. These are instances exemplifying the connection between the local culture and the local materials. Workshops developed from a local base are more likely to succeed. It is easier for artists to explore the connection and its implications, and thereby make works speaking to the local culture and materials.

The first ironworks (Takao Ironworks) in Taiwan opened in Kaohsiung in 1919, initiating its career of heavy industry. Since the Ten Major Construction Projects expedited its development of steel industry and petrochemical industry in the 1970s, it has been flourishing and supporting Taiwan as a city of heavy industry. While the industries were growing rapidly, culture and arts were given far less attention in Kaohsiung than in Taipei. But as I visited the 2014 KISISF in the Pier-2 and the past KISISF works in its fan-shaped park, it struck me that Kaohsiung has not wanted to mimic Taipei. Nor does it have to. Aside from the Pier-2 Art Center, Kaohsiung Museum of Military Departments Village, and Wei Wu Ying Center for the Arts opened after the Kaohsiung Museum of Fine Arts, the Kaohsiung International Container Arts Festival and KISISF that alternated every year with each other were noticeably determined to quest after the local spirit of Kaohsiung.

3. Creation and exchange are the focus of the workshop. It is a routine for the artists to work in public, whether they enjoy conversing with the visitors or not. As long as the visitors are able to see the process of creation, and the artists are conscious of that, meanings begin to proliferate.

Apart from working in public, it is also important for the artists to exchange ideas with and understand each other, look for mutual friends, and strengthen their connections. Artists are often alone in the studio, but the workshop in which they work and live together, help and talk to each other, generates a sense of partnership among them, turning them into comrades and good friends. They have the opportunity to explore foreign cultures, and the friendship may contribute to introducing them to workshops and cultural activities in the foreign countries. The Department of Sculpture, National Taiwan University of Arts, had invited Erőss István, with whom a professor acquainted in a workshop, as one of the visiting professors. It manifests the significance of the workshop, in which the artists watch and be watched, in the international cultural exchange. In the workshops I attended in Japan and Europe, the artists were often asked to introduce their works and countries after dinner to promote mutual understanding. The "Meeting the Artists" forum in the KISISF extended the exchange to include the visitors, and even recorded it in written form. In the other KISISF forum "From Workshop to Art Festival: Art Production, City Marketing and Cultural Action", I exchanged ideas with the other panel members concerning the current condition of Sanyi International Woodcarving Art Festival and its workshop. Workshops, mostly sculpture workshops, attempt to invigorate the local cultural atmosphere. While Kaohsiung emphasizes city marketing and cultural activities, Sanyi is occupied by the idea of art production, and relies on the over one million visitors of the festival to support its tourism industry.

4. The theme and aim of the workshop as a strategy to attract attention should be simple, direct and consistent, making it easier to be concentrated and advertised. The theme of every KISISF -- "Steel Super" (2014), "Steel, Love" (2012), "Steel Is Just Fine" (2010), "Metallicity. Radiance: The Temperature of City" (2008), "The Metallicity Style" (2006), "Welding Together. Crossing Boundary" (2004), and "Steel City. Sculpture Hope" (2002) -- has perceptibly demonstrated the close relation between materials and region, and the intention to forge the image of Kaohsiung with steel and iron sculptures. The biennial workshop has been conveying the historical message of the city.

5. The obligation and social responsibility to publicize the work. The process of creation is publicized not only for the visitors, but also for the fellow artists, who are the best interlocutors to exchange ideas, feelings, techniques, and skills of using equipments, etc. The experience is beneficial to both the artists and the visitors. Exhibiting the works is also an important part of the process. If they are sold or collected by individuals, the workshop may lose its appeal. This is why the works made for the KISISF workshops are everywhere in the Pier-2, and characterize it as a locus of art. The sculptures made in the workshops of the Hualien International Stone Sculpture Festival are also installed in various tourist spots and main streets to entertain the drivers' eyes. It will be a pity if they are not publicized.

The KISISF has had positive impacts on the development of local culture over the years, as Kaohsiung is transforming from a cultural desert into a capital of culture. The impressions the foreign artists have of the port city is also a kind of civil diplomacy. As I wrote, I realized that workshops are an influential art activity. I am reaiiy looking forward to seeing the artworks brought us by KISISF in the future.

第七屆高雄國際鋼雕藝術節活動報導

撰文／劉子嘉

　　鋼鐵產業之於高雄這個重工業城市發展的重要性使鋼雕藝術節與貨櫃藝術節已然成為高雄在藝術界的重要標誌，自 2002 年創始至今已第七屆的高雄國際鋼雕藝術節，本屆策展人劉俊蘭引用馬列主義中的「無限上綱」將其延伸為「無限上鋼」，以「超越既定」翻轉其原有的負面意涵，藉開放的藝術想像與多元詮釋，重新刻寫擴展與鋼鐵的新美學關係。劉俊蘭表示，第七屆高雄國際鋼雕藝術節要以「限地」、「限材」、「限時」之大型鋼鐵創作營，開啟遼闊視野的國際想像，以重量級的作品，挑戰藝術無限可能。在以重工業奠基的高雄舉行這個城市藝術節，「鋼鐵限定」的鮮明路線與獨特屬性，企圖以「超越既定」而「無限擴展」的創作挑戰，擴展與鋼鐵之間超越工業的聯繫，開展這場充滿鋼鐵港都特質的藝術盛會。

　　由高雄市政府文化局、財團法人東和鋼鐵文化基金會與策展人劉俊蘭等攜手合作，邀請六位分別來自義大利的瑞卡多·柯德羅（Riccardo Cordero）、俄羅斯的尼古拉·波利斯基（Nikolay Polissky）、中國的尚曉風、日本的前田哲明、台灣的梁任宏、劉柏村等六位國際級鋼雕藝術家，接下「無限上鋼」

之三大挑戰：歷年來最大創作基地、最重作品量體以及跨國藝術家與在地技術團隊共同合作。

　　本屆高雄國際鋼雕藝術節創作基地位於駁二藝術特區淺三碼頭，同時為高雄港第三船渠，並緊臨西臨港線自行車道。在如此開闊且左擁右抱海港景色與社區人文的環境中進行創作，開放性及與親民性一直以來都是鋼雕藝術節作品不可或缺的特色，也是每到駁二藝術特區的民眾必訪的打卡點。而鋼雕所使用的巨型鋼材、焊槍切割器、起重吊具等，與藝術家就在你眼前施工的限地製作形式，也突破了大眾對藝術的認知。

　　財團法人東和鋼鐵文化基金會於 2011 年成立之際，即希望成為將台灣藝術家推向國際的藝術平台。自 2012 年「全民大戀鋼」開始加入鋼雕藝術節，本屆更提供超過 120 噸的回收鋼鐵材料作為創作素材。2014 年「無限上鋼」採國際創作營模式，共有來自歐亞五國六位藝術家，在歷時約三個星期的創作時間，和由蔡坤霖、鄭陽晟以及宇建形象有限公司組成的在地技術團隊，共同打造出七件巨型鋼雕作品。

位於展區的第一件作品是來自日本的前田哲明，以擅長的捲曲鋼鐵片材重複構成立體組件，看似粗獷卻又不失細膩的風格曾在 2001 年獲得日本當代雕塑雙年展首獎、2007 年札幌雕刻美術館頒授本鄉新獎，並於日本及英國兩地舉辦過多次個展。前田哲明驚訝於高雄這個海港城市與日本橫濱如此相似，本次於高雄國際鋼雕藝術節的作品《無題 2015 ── 高雄》在確立了錐形骨幹主結構後，利用不規則剪裁的舊鋼管片有韻律地堆疊出富有生機的形象。看似堅硬卻像溫柔的樹葉一片片包覆構成的組件，下方開放式空間則邀請民眾進入作品，用不同的視角去體察藝術與世界的距離。

緊鄰在旁的是俄羅斯的尼古拉・波利斯基由台灣風俗民情所發想的聖火及錨鏈機，尼古拉・波利斯基與其子依凡・波利斯基（Ivan Polissky）為本次旅台藝術家中唯一的父子檔。尼古拉・波利斯基在俄羅斯獨立策畫了莫斯科 Nikola-Lenivets 雕塑公園，將自己與駐村藝術家的作品結合當地環境，形成大型地景。因此，對於高雄國際鋼雕藝術節有政府與企業的支持，特別讚賞。在對台灣人文歷史背景有了初步認識後，尼古拉・波利斯基構思了兩件較為具象的作品，第一件作品《錨鏈機》利用一大捆回收的舊鐵鏈，一圈一圈地捆繞在一個重達 5 噸的大型工業輪軸上。在高雄港附近可見的金屬機具尺寸都要比我們日常生活中所見的放大許多倍，在《錨鏈機》前，觀眾彷彿變成了小人國的一員。第二件作品《聖火》的靈感來自於常民生活中的金屬火爐，雖有著西方的外貌，卻不難發現細節處充滿著熟悉的在地元素，高聳入天的雙柱造型也增添了作品的神聖性，確實運作後的《聖火》亦有以往雕塑所沒有的實際功能。尼古拉・波利斯基希望透過他的作品，並在《聖火》燃燒時，緊扣高雄人鋼鐵般堅毅精神與高雄港船舶、重工業城市的深刻連結。

有「鐵器時代的巨人」美稱的義大利藝術家瑞卡多・柯德羅，曾任教於艾爾伯提納美術學院，並曾兩度受邀在威尼斯雙年展中舉辦個人展覽。帶著超過半世紀的豐厚創作經歷，瑞卡多・柯德羅為高雄打造了一座極富幾何美感的作品《天上大誌》，仿

若一個巨型機械錶零件座落人間。雕塑主體由兩段經過精準計算的 C 型弧構成一個開放的圓，作品的「線性」形式巧妙地將圓解構再建構，體積雖大卻具有相當的開放感，使鋼材呈現少見的輕盈，與具有固實量體的雕塑類型不同的，並非是「佔有」而是「解放」空間，因而更得以與遼闊的空間對話，也在作品與觀眾之間建立更積極的關係。

發現拆解自橋樑建築和大型機械的廢鋼鐵組件，這些曾承載極大重力而在回收時又經巨大力量扭曲變形的材料時，中國藝術家尚曉風找到了他《海之夢》的作品靈魂。描繪著豎立於 S 形的基座上，以厚鋼板焊接拼組而成的圓盤，宛如飛碟亦似某種海貝；在其作品上方，扭曲的 H 鋼樑，向空中延展，有如緞帶，也像浮雲，更召喚出東方禪意。尚曉風畢業自北京的中央美院，旅澳創作多年後回到母校任教，為藝術而藝術一直是尚曉風的創作中心，影響他在抽象與具象的思維中不斷流變。

作品經常緊扣著人與自然意象之台灣藝術家劉柏村，曾參與多屆高雄鋼雕藝術節，亦擔任過東和鋼鐵廠駐廠藝術家，創作營期間完成的《雲端漫步》利用凝結成片狀、外形輪廓不規則的煉鋼爐渣，切割表現高掛於空中的流水行雲線狀鋼條；並以厚實鋼板裁切出鋪於地面的雲朵，還有高聳矗立、並比成群的林木身影，構築出一條仿若古木參天的「雲端步道」。劉柏村對鋼材特性的熟悉，讓他將工業化對人類與自然帶來的影響所做的一番省思完整呈現在其作品裡。《雲端漫步》置放的位置旁邊即是一列綠樹，《雲端漫步》與之並列，竟也看似和諧無違。

《What is 花枝？》該是這系列作品中，名稱最抽象，作品本體卻最為具象的一件。《What is 花枝？》出自台灣藝術家梁任宏之手，梁任宏以創作自然力運動的作品著名，亦是高雄鋼雕藝術節元老級藝術家。構思《What is 花枝？》之際，乃幻想它是一隻來自外星抑或海底的八足生物，有著四隻會隨風擺動的手足，頗富童趣；而沉重的鋼鐵材料，在經過精密的計算，海風一吹，竟也可輕盈地隨風律動。作品完成後，主辦單位將之用高空吊車吊至大義倉庫屋頂置放，唯有走路不低頭，才能發現這件半掛天空的驚奇作品。

從工業物質的生產到文化的創造與革新，從侷限的突破到框架的挑戰，從舊物質中翻轉出的新視野；與高雄在地產業緊密結合的鋼雕藝術節，在作品完成之際，創作的腳步卻從沒有停過，港邊的海風與烈日每天都為這七座鋼雕著上鏽色，令鋼雕作品比初完工之際更顯鮮明生動。「從土地長出來的文化最感人」乃本土劇團金枝演社的座右銘，而鋼雕藝術節正是為土生土長的高雄文化開出一朵最耀眼的花。

On the 7ᵗʰ Kaohsiung International Steel and Iron Sculpture Festival

Liu Tzu-Chia

The significance of steel and iron industry in the industrial development of Kaohsiung has made the Kaohsiung International Steel and Iron Sculpture Festival (KISISF) and the Kaohsiung International Container Arts Festival signature art events in the city. The KISISF was launched in 2002. "Steel Super" as the theme of the 7ᵗʰ KISISF was adapted by the curator Liu Chun-Lan from a Chinese term of Marxism-Leninism to invert the negative implication, stimulate imagination and interpretations, and re-shape and enrich the aesthetic relationship between Kaohsiung and steel and iron. By the workshop's limits of location, medium and time, Liu Chun-Lan intended to open up a broader international vision, and pose challenges to large-scale works. Drawing on the industrial context of Kaohsiung, the city festival's distinct "steel and iron limited" character and unique attributes strove to transcend and expand, to inform the tie between steel and iron and industry with an innovative spirit.

The Bureau of Cultural Affairs, Kaohsiung City Government, Tung Ho Steel Foundation, and the curator Liu Chun-Lan cooperated and invited six internationally renowned steel sculptors -- Riccardo Cordero (Italy), Nikolay Polissky (Russia), Noriaki Maeda (Japan), Shang Xiao-Feng (China), Liang Jen-Hung (Taiwan), and Liu Po-Chun (Taiwan) -- to respond to the three challenges of "Steel Super": It had the largest base, demanded the heaviest work, and called for the joint effort of foreign artists and the domestic technical team.

The 2014 KISISF was based in Dock 3, the Pier 2 Art Center, which is the third quay of Kaohsiung port next to the West Side Harbor Bikeway. The

past KISISF works made in this wide landscape embracing the harbor and the human environment have been characterized by being open and accessible, and are the favorite check-in points for the visitors. The gigantic steel materials, welders, and cranes required for making the steel sculptures, as well as the on-site creation process, have also refreshed people's view of art.

Tung Ho Steel Foundation was established in 2011, in hope of introducing the Taiwanese artists to the international stage. Having participated in the KISISF since the 2012 "Steel, Love", it offered 120 recycled steel and iron for the 2014 KISISF. In the "Steel Super" workshop, 6 European and Asian artists created 7 monumental sculptures in about 3 weeks, supported by the local technical team led by Tsai Kun-Lin, Cheng Yang-Cheng, and Yu-Jian CO., LTD Taiwan.

The first sculpture in display was by Noriaki Maeda, who layered curvy steel sheets into a solid composition, a familiar form in his oeuvre. His rusty yet refined style had won him the first prize of the 2001 Contemporary Japanese Sculpture Biennale and the 2007 Hongo Shin Prize from the Sapporo Museum of Sculpture, and he had exhibited exten-

sively in Japan and England. Amazed by the similarity between Kaohsiung and Yokohama, Maeda cut and layered irregular parts from old steel tubes in a rhythmic way to build the organic cone structure of Untitled 2015 -- Kaohsiung. The seemingly hard structure with the soft and opulent image of leaves and an opening in its lower part invited the visitors to view the world in a different perspective.

Adjacent to it is the sacred fire and capstan inspired by the Taiwanese culture and made by the only father-son pair of the KISISF artists -- Nikolay Polissky and his son Ivan Polissky. As the organizer of Nikola-Lenivets, Nikolay Polissky merged his and other artists' works with the local environment as part of a larger landscape. Impressed by the support of the government and the industries for KISISF, he responded to the historical and cultural background of the city with two concrete images. Braadspil applied a huge load of recycled chain cables to bundle a large capstan weighed 5 tons. The metal machines and equipments in the

port are much larger than normally seen in the daily life. Braadspil seemed to turnethe visitors into Lilliputians. Sacred Fire was inspired by the incense burners commonly seen in the local life. The Western contour is filled with the local details, while the two towering columns exhumed a sense of sacredness. Sacred Fire also has a practical function that other works do not. Polissky hoped that the fire burning on top of the columns may strengthen and invigorate the tie between the port and the steel-like will of the residents of the industrial city.

Praised as "Iron Giant", Riccardo Cordero had taught in the Accademia Albertina di Belle Arti di Torino, and held two solo exhibitions in la Biennale di Venezia. With a career of over half a century, Cordero infused "Grande segno nel cielo, 2014" with a geometric beauty, as if it is an enormous machine part falling from the sky. The sculpture consists in two C-shapes ingeniously forming into an open circle deconstructed and reconstructed by the lines. Prodigious, open, and light, which is rarely seen in steel works, it liberated rather than occupied the space as other substantial works did, and thereby established a dialogue with the vast space, a more dynamic interaction with the visitors.

Scrap parts from bridges and large machines extremely pressured and distorted prior to and in the process of recycling instilled a soul into Shang Xiao-Feng's "Dreams of Ocean". The saucer welded from thick steel sheets erected on the S-shaped podium looks like a flying object or a sea shell, above which a twisted H-beam stretched upward like ribbons or clouds, evoking a sense of Zen. After working in

Australia for years, Shang retuned to teach at the Central Academy of Fine Arts in Beijing where he graduated. Art for art's sake as the core of his career has affected his style to constantly alternat between the abstract and the figurative.

Liu Po-Chun is a regular participator of KISISF and was an artist-in-residence in Tung Ho Steel Factory whose oeuvre reflects on the relationship between humans and nature. In Roaming over Clouds made for the 2014 KISISF, irregular sheets of steel slag were cut into clouds in the sky, and thick steel plates were cut into clouds on the ground and soaring trees in rows, to construct a "trail in clouds". Liu's familiarity with steel enabled him to fully address his concern of how humans have affected nature. Roaming over Clouds seemed to be in perfect harmony with the neighboring trees.

What is a Cuttlefish? has the most abstract title and the most figurative appearance. Known for kinetic works, Liang Jen-Hung, who is also one of the earliest participators of KISISF, imagined What is a Cuttlefish? to be an alien or a cephalopod with eight tentacles from the deep ocean and four horns flying in the wind, a creature from the fairytale. After precise calculation, the heavy steel moved to the sea wind. As it was completed, it was moved to the roof of DaYi Warehouse by an aerial lift vehicle. Only when you looked up could you find this amazing work hanging in the air.

From industrial production to cultural creation and innovation, from transcending the limits to challenging the established rules, from old materials to new visions, the KISISF works closely related to the local industry have not stopped developing after the artists left. The sea wind and the blazing sun in the port have been coloring the seven sculptures, and animating them with a vivacious life. As the motto of the Golden Bough Theatre "Culture born from the native land is most touching" suggests, the KISISF is the most dazzling flower cradled by the local culture of Kaohsiung.

參展藝術家
Artist

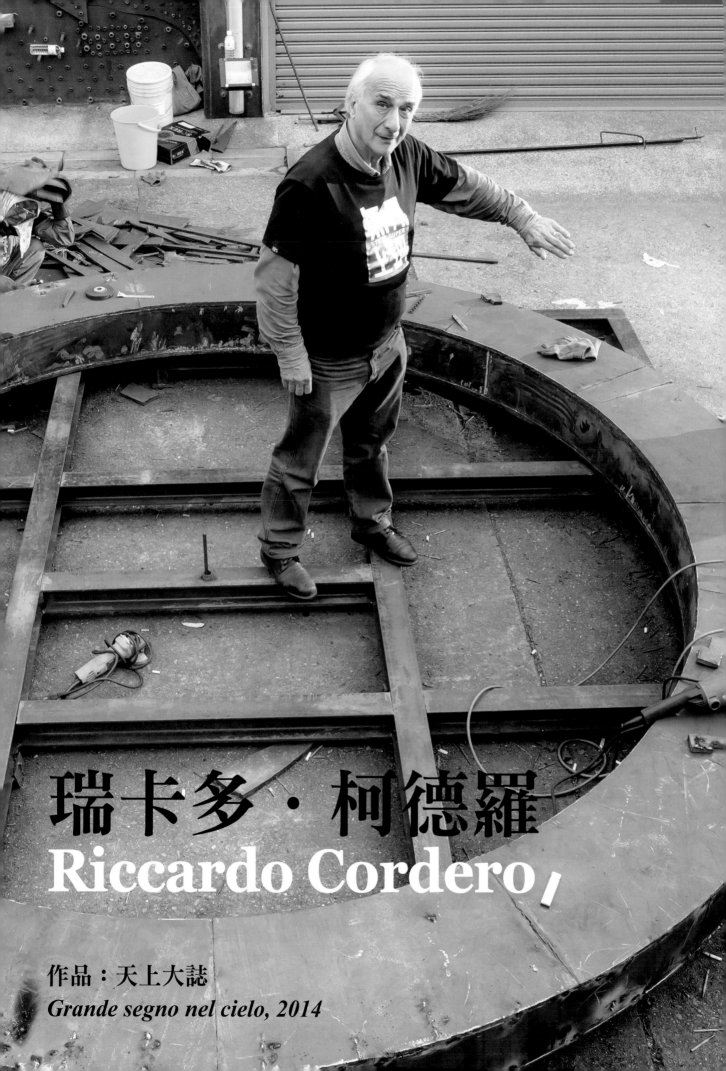

瑞卡多・柯德羅
Riccardo Cordero

作品：天上大誌
Grande segno nel cielo, 2014

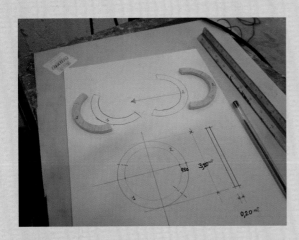

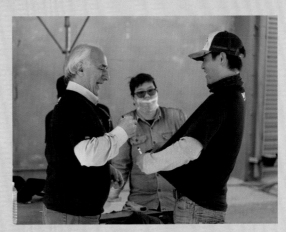

義大利藝術家瑞卡多・柯德羅，曾任教於艾爾伯提納美術學院（Accademia Albertina di Belle Arti di Torino）。在他已超過半世紀的藝術生涯中，不但個展無數，更頻頻現身於重要的國際大展，甚至兩度受邀在指標性的威尼斯雙年展中舉辦個人展覽。他的早期創作結合了碎片般的有機形態與規則的幾何造型；近年作品則多以粗細一致的長條金屬方柱彎曲成形，在空間中畫出既見理性秩序又富層次韻律的立體結構。柯德羅長期投入金屬雕塑的創作，創造力豐沛。在他2013 年的藝術家聯展中，策展人 Martina Corgnati 曾以「鐵器時代的巨人」來定位他驚人的藝術能量與不凡的藝術表現。

1942 生於義大利庫內奧省阿爾巴

艾爾伯提納美術學院學士

Sandro Cherchi 學院雕塑碩士學位

Franco Garelli 學院解剖碩士學位

個展

2013　Riccardo Cordero 個展，鐵器時代的巨人 1960-2013，策展人 Martina Corgnati，
　　　嘉布遣會修道院，卡拉廖市庫內奧省

2011　Riccardo Cordero 個展，法拉利藝廊 Ferrari Art Gallery，沃韋，瑞士

聯展

2012　藝術博覽會，芙尼藝廊 Galleria Forni，波隆那

2011　湖國際藝術雕塑創作營，桂林愚自樂園，上海，中國

2010　地中海當代藝術，Carlini Cordero Licata，地中海阿格德海水浴場，法國 Art

Riccardo Cordero

had taught in the Accademia Albertina di Belle Arti di Torino,and during his art career of over half a century, he has exhibited frequently in major international art venues. Cordero had been invited twice to stage his solo exhibition in la Biennale di Venezia, one of the most significant art events throughout the world. The artist's early works integrated fragmentary and organic shapes into regular geometric forms. In recent years he began to bend metal tubes of identical dimensions into curves to constitute rational, rhythmic and multi-layered structures. Devoted in metal sculpture for a long time, Cordero never loses his vigor and creativity. In an anthological exhibition in 2013, curator Martina Corgnati used the words Iron Giant to praise his amazing art energy and extraordinary accomplishment.

Biography

Born in Alba, in the north-west Italian province of Cuneo, in 1942

taking his diploma at the Albertine Academy of Fine Arts in Turin in 1965.

masters degree at Sandro Cherchi for sculpture

masters degree for anatomy Franco Garelli

Solo Exhibition

2013   Riccardo Cordero Iron Giants from 1960 to 2013, curated by Martina Corgnati, Filatoio e
        Giardoino del Convento dei Cappuccini, Caraglio (Cuneo)

2011   Riccardo Cordero, Gall. Ferrari, Vevey (Svizzera, Swiss)

Group Exhibition

2012   Arte Fiera 2012, Galleria Forni, Bologna

2011   Exhibition Sculpture Workshop 2011, Shanghai Sculpture Park, Shanghai (China)

2010   Art contemporain del Mediterraneo, Carlini Cordero Licata, Capd'Adge, (France)

創作理念

　　以流動的不穩定平衡狀態現身，這個作品重新找到了創新感，也找到了靜態素材與環境對話關係中那未經探索的空間係數。作品主體內部和外部無法界定的遼闊等待著標記出現，以測量它無邊無際的種種形式可能。

　　這個雕刻作品的意義在於它奮力打破了幾何議題，透過空間環環相繞的手法，讓構圖的平衡在欲開未開、欲闔未闔之間呈現出動能感，永無止息，並不時隱喻更大的維度。

　　雕刻家在圓中追尋的並非形式的純粹本質，而是試圖讓圓永遠脫離那完美的、可預測的弧線，以斷裂平面近乎混亂的縱橫交錯讓人記起超越既有空間、在空無中的展翅飛翔。

　　用出現在每一個作品中，而且每一次都不同的線條的對峙和解構的律動，表現出對懸置形式的崇仰，也指出了這個作品可能的自鳴性。所謂自鳴性，除了物理進程中散解的斷簡殘編外，更重要的是能夠捕捉到源自素材核心的空氣輕盈感的那個永恆場域。

　　張力、對位與構圖決定了看得見的主體形塑過程，那既是作品本身，也與未知、抽象本能、具象記憶、結構理性和情感違逆同時共存。這樣的辯證關係，在柯德洛的《天上大誌，2014》作品

中顯而易見。相較於其他對其形塑的界定，這個作品的懸置感更為鮮明，因而將沉重轉化為輕盈，將量體轉化為空無和無邊界的一場遊戲。

　　支撐結構的幾何形式能讓人細細體會外型輪廓呈現的張力，而所有支微末節的無用之物又再度融入外型輪廓中，這似乎是為了將爆發力限制在一定的形狀之中。

　　組合一個圓和拆解一個圓，變成同時進行的一個動作，受思維所控，擺脫了原始量體的靜態功能，尋找是否有失去平衡的可能性……。

　　圓形的滾動原則對柯德洛極為重要，可説是一個先驗的參涉，在他的想像世界中這個概念是堅定不移的。圓是各種關係持續改變的一個場，圓雖然不是穩定的，卻變成能從周遭獲得能量的一個工具，彷彿在聆聽世界的聲音……。

摘錄自 Claudio Cerritelli 專文

Creation Motive

This sculpture is innovative because of its co-existing energies, which demonstrates an unstable balance as well as the correlation between the material and the space. The spacious energy flow within and surrounding the sculpture awaits to be defined and to be measured as it shows the unlimited potential of an artwork.

The soul of this sculpture is that it breaks the framework of geometric shapes. The sculpture demonstrates a dynamic flow through the overlapping geometric shapes in the space, displaying a dynamic balance within the opening and closing circles. The dynamic balance goes on as the audience approach, implying a larger scale of energy flow every now and then.

The message that the sculptor hopes to pass down through the cracking and chaotic display is that he hopes the audience can recall a specific moment in their lives that has long been forgotten. He hopes to free the spirits of any individual, let them soar into the sky. The geometric shapes of the sculpture are not the usual perfect rounded circles, it is something beyond the forms that the sculptor has been pursuing.

Every single piece of artwork has different appearance. Different shapes of lines produce different degrees of dynamic energy. The lines of this sculpture clash against one another invisibly, decompose the structure of the sculpture and display their own characteristics. During the process of creating a sculpture, sculptors carve on the material, whittle it and capture the feeling of airy lightness within the material. An eternal atmosphere can therefore be presented to the audience.

The tension, para-position of the shapes and the composition are the key elements that make an artwork alive. The artwork itself should be able to connect with the unforeseen future, the abstract thinking and the memories of an individual. A dialectic relation is obvious in Riccardo Cordero's Grande segno nel cielo, 2014. Comparing to the lines of other pieces of sculptures, Grande segno nel cielo, 2014 displays a more vivid image through the suspended geometric shapes. The whole creation process was like a game, transforming the sense of heaviness originated from the steel into a feeling of airy lightness.

The geometric forms that support the sculpture invite the audience to dwell on the dynamic tension from within. Any details considered to be insignificant blend in the sculpture perfectly, as if the dynamic energy was locked within the contours.

In this sculpture, assembling and disassembling the parts of the circles seem to be an action happening at the same time. It's human's mind that determines the meaning of any artwork, not the resting shapes. The sculptor looks for the possibility of an existing unbalanced world by way of his sculpture.

The traditional impression that circles present is extremely important for Riccardo Cordero, as if it is a priori deeply rooted in his mind. Circle is the basic form of any transformation. Although it does not demonstrate the same stable feeling as other shapes do, it can be seen as a vehicle absorbing energy from its surroundings, or in a serene position listening to what the world has to say…

Extracted from Claudio Cerritelli's article

尼古拉・波利斯基
Nikolay Polissky

作品：錨鏈機 & 聖火
Braadspil & Sacred Fire

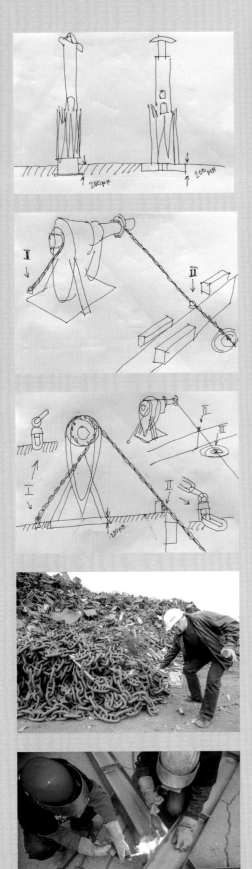

俄國藝術家尼古拉 · 波利斯基擅長利用巨型雕塑介入戶外空間，特別是自然環境。他的作品常是量體驚人、規模宏偉，直逼建築或山丘的巍峨尺度。波利斯基擬仿、變造知名建築形式的系列創作，尤其聞名。他屢次受邀於歐美各國展出，2008 年並曾代表俄羅斯參加第十一屆威尼斯建築雙年展。波利斯基一次次挑戰、突破極限的大型創作，不僅迴響著人類歷史與文化，也交會著自然與人工。它們每每震撼人們的視覺印象，更衝擊人們的身體感官，屢屢召喚觀眾既細膩幽微又澎湃填膺的複雜情感，讓人矛盾地同時感受人類的渺小與巨大。

簡歷
1957 年生於莫斯科
畢業於穆西那列寧葛拉德高等工業藝術學院

個展
2009　MUDAM 盧森堡現代美術館，盧森堡
2008　俄羅斯展覽館，第六屆威尼斯建築雙年展，威尼斯
1997　俄羅斯藝術之家，烏哥拉河的二十個角度

聯展
2012　康丁斯基藝術獎藝術家提名展，莫斯科
2011　Bêtes Off 巴黎古監獄，巴黎
　　　俄羅斯貧窮藝術，米蘭當代藝術館
2010　第五屆俄羅斯年度當代藝術創新獎提名展，
　　　NCCA 國立當代藝術中心，莫斯科

Nikolay Polissky
likes to present large sculpture in outdoor space, especially in nature. Many of his works consist tremendous volumes to parallel the grandeur of man-made or nature-made architecture, such as a precipitous mountain. Polissky is especially known by his imitation and transformation of famous architectural works and had been invited to show his sculpture in Europe and the U.S. frequently. In 2008 he represented Russia and exhibited in the 11th architecture show of la Biennale di Venezia. Polissky never ceases challenging the limitations of gigantic projects in order to address historical and cultural issues under both artificial environment and natural conditions. His presentation never fails to amaze the audience visually and physically. At the same time they evoke our delicate and obscure feelings that are further complicated by the rushing momentum in them, and we are introduced the conflicting experience of being trivial and grand at the same time.

Born in Moscow, 1957

Graduated from Leningrad Higher industrial-art school of Muhina.

Solo Exhibition

2009   Museum of Contemprorary Art of Luxembourg "MUDAM", Luxembourg

2008   Russian Exhibition Hall, XI Venice Biennale of Architecture, Venice

1997   "Twenty views of the river Ugra", Central House of Artists, Moscow

Group Exhibition

2012   Exhibition of the nominees on Kandinsky Prize 2012, Moscow

2011   "Bêtes Off ", Conciergerie, Paris

      "Russian Povera", Padiglione d' Arte Contemporanea, Milano

2010   Exhibition of the nominees for V Russian Annual "Innovation" Award,
NCCA, Moscow

《錨鏈機》創作理念

　　這件作品，是為了紀念高雄的舊港灣。其中的鎖鏈，不論在實質上或概念上，都連結了高雄舊港灣的命脈——海洋與工業港。

　　創作這件作品的靈感，最初是出現於創作者造訪「東和鋼鐵」的廠區；那裡堆積著回收的舊金屬、水管、建築原料、以及廢棄不用的舊車，而他在那些物品裡注意到兩件特別的物品：一大綑錨鍊，以及一個沉重的機械輪軸。他非常意外地發現，這兩件物品能夠和諧地搭配在一起，因此，他只剩下一個工作，就是尋找一個方式，把這兩件物品的組合與隱藏在背後的情感連結起來。

　　時至今日，人們已經不再需要重工業了。重工業被新興科技與更輕巧的材料取代，體積縮小而不減其效力，因此這些巨大而鏽蝕的物件最終都被送進了熔爐中。它們唯一再生的機會，就是透過藝術家為它們創造新的生命，將它們塑造成一個紀念碑，紀念那些創造了這些鐵鍊、並且利用這些鐵鍊在海上乘風破浪的人們。

　　這件藝術品使用了船上機械構造的概念，代表著升降船錨的輪軸。現在，這個作品被放在碼頭，鐵鍊的其中一端深深沒入海水中，好像那裡隱藏了一個珍貴的秘密。這個隱晦的連結彷彿平衡了整個作品，讓它成為一個回憶的象徵——乘載了一切、卻又有些朦朧不清。

Creation Motive (Braadspil)

This piece of artwork commemorates the old harbor city of Kaohsiung. The chains, physically or conceptually, link to the lifeblood of Kaohsiung's old harbor-- the ocean and the industrial harbors.

The inspiration comes from the pile of recycled metal, water pipes, construction materials and old vehicles stacked in the works of Tung Ho Steel Enterprise. When the sculptor first visited the works, he noticed there were two special objects within the materials: a huge chain cable and a heavy capstan. He found out surprisingly that these two pieces match perfectly. Therefore, the only work left to do was to find a way to demonstrate the connection between the two materials and the history they carry.

Heavy industry is no longer in need in modern society. It has been replaced with new technology and lighter materials that have smaller volume but the same efficiency. Those large and rusty materials end up melting in the furnace. Through the hands of the artist, those materials can be endued with a new soul and be displayed once again. I shaped these recycled materials as a monument in memory of those who invented these chains and those who used the chains to ride and split the waves.

This artwork involves a mechanic structure of a ship-- an axle used for casting and raising anchors. At present, this artwork is being displayed at the harbor with one end of the chain deeply submerged in the sea as if there was treasure hidden underneath. This connection somehow creates a balance for this artwork, which can be seen as a vague symbol of the heavy memories from the past.

《聖火》創作理念

　　把在地的象徵具體化的呈現在作品裡，是尼古拉‧波利斯基的作品中不可或缺的一部分。現今的世界正逐漸變得相似──身處在任何城市中，好像都沒有什麼區別。因此，在這其中找到一些日常生活的珍貴痕跡，便成為了創作者的靈感來源。當他在節慶期間造訪高雄的大街小巷時，這些私人空間中最值得注意的金屬建物，便是那些用於宗教儀式的金爐、烘烤食物的烤爐、或甚至是焚燒木頭的火爐。這個觀察結果告訴我們，這些露天的爐火仍然在人們的日常生活中扮演極為重要的角色，甚至是整個國家的統一文化。

　　這位創作者的主要創作原則,就是把當地居民融入他的創作之中。他鼓勵他的創作助理們保有自己的創作獨立性,而不是全然按照他的意思來進行創作。波利斯基深信,這些透過不同人的手創造而成、再聚集起來的作品,能夠在新興類型的雕塑中擦出強而有力的火花。身兼藝術家與工作室技術指導的鄭陽晟先生,他曾經為主辦單位設計了許多不同種的火爐和烤箱;這次他也協助波利斯基完成了這個作品。他對於這些火爐的熱情是整個作品最初的靈感來源,而他在工程方面的專長也是成品製作過程當中不可或缺的一環。

　　這個作品的核心想法,是將它塑造一個真實可用的雕塑,讓在地居民能夠在見到它的瞬間就與之產生連結、將它當作生活中的一部分,而且在特定的時間點可以於駁二點燃。在當地協作者鄭先生的幫助下,這個欄杆狀的火爐終於能順利達成這個理想。

Creation Motive (Sacred Fire)

Concretizing local features in artworks is the principle of Nikolay Polissky. The world now has been blended into one huge community where distinctions between cities seem to be hazy. In response to this situation, the sculptor looked for cultural tracks within daily life that people have left behind. When he visited Kaohsiung in times of festivals, the most attractive metal objects he saw were incense burners, stoves cooking food and fire pits burning wood. This reveals that those outdoor burners still play an important role in people's daily life. They represent a deeply rooted tradition of the country.

The main creative motive of the sculptor is to involve local inhabitants in his artwork. He encouraged his assistants to uphold their independence during the process of creating rather than following his instructions. He believes that artworks being created through involving inspiration from various people can create a spark. Mr. Cheng Yang-Cheng, the artist and technical instructor of the atelier, has assisted in designing numerous burners and ovens for festivals. This time he has taken part in Polissky's creation as well. The passion he holds towards the burners is where the inspiration came from initially, along with his expertise in engineering are necessary in the creating process.

The creative motive of this sculpture is to produce a piece of artwork that is practical but also creates a connection with the audience spontaneously when they see it. The sculptor hopes this sculpture becomes a part of people's life and that it can be lit up on Pier-2 at specific times. With the assistance of Mr. Cheng, the burner with double steel tubes has been created successfully.

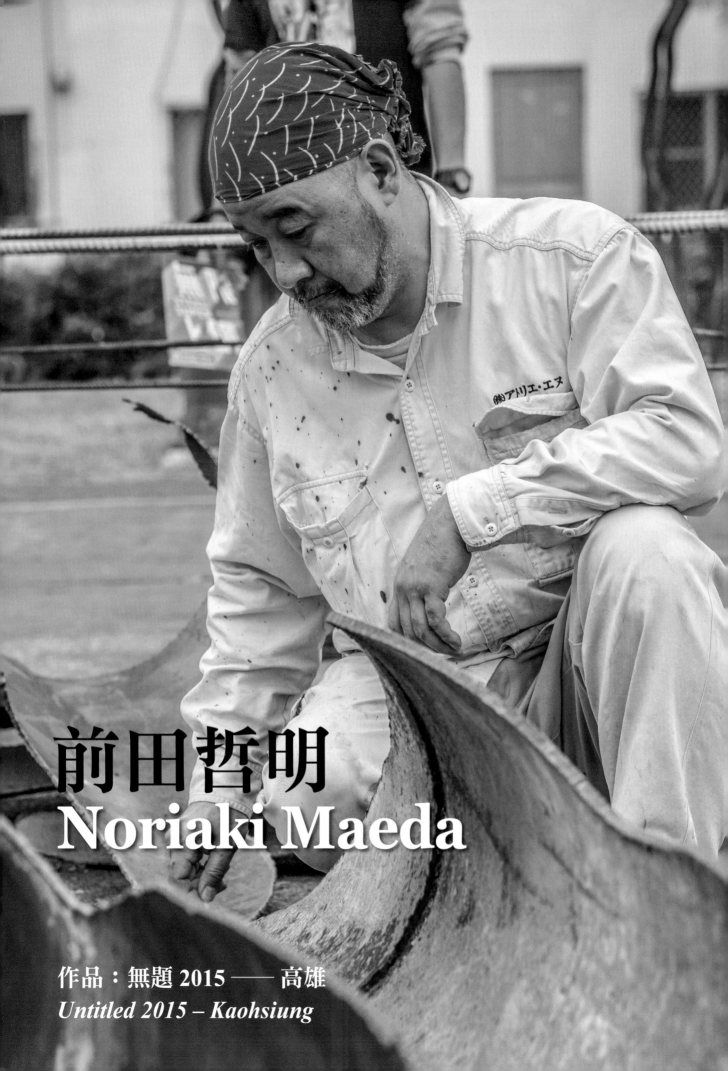

前田哲明
Noriaki Maeda

作品：無題 2015 —— 高雄
Untitled 2015 – Kaohsiung

現生活於東京的前田哲明，曾旅居英倫數年，在英國及日本兩地多次舉辦個展。他的作品屢屢於雕塑競賽中脫穎而出，就如在 2001 年日本當代雕塑雙年展贏得首獎、2007 年獲札幌雕刻美術館頒授本鄉新獎。前田哲明的作品風格鮮明，特別以鋼鐵雕塑馳名。他常以有如破碎薄頁的捲曲鋼鐵作為基本元素，重複組構成立體造型，作品表面鏽色緻密，但卻也粗糙而富陳舊感，宛如一方古代遺址或自然廢墟。

簡歷

1961 年生於東京
東京國立大學美術與音樂學系碩士
東京國立大學美術與音樂學系博士
1997-2001 旅居倫敦
現居東京

個展

2014　H 藝廊，東京，日本

2013　COEXSIST-TOKYO 藝廊，東京，日本

2008　秋山畫廊，東京，日本
　　　愛宕山藝術作品，東京，日本

2007　橫濱港邊藝廊 Yokohama Portside Gallery，橫濱，日本
　　　本鄉新記念札幌彫刻美術館，北海道，日本

聯展

2009　新潟市「水土藝術祭」，新潟市，日本

2007　文化廳藝術家在外研修制度 40 周年記念展，東京，日本

Noriaki Maeda

lives in Tokyo now. He had lived in London for years and had exhibited in the U.K. and Japan frequently. Maeda's art stands out in many sculpture competitions, he was the recipient of the first prize of the 2001 Contemporary Japanese Sculpture Biennale and the 2007 Hongo Shin Prize from the Sapporo Museum of Sculpture. Maeda's iron sculpture has an unusual style; he likes to make use of thin and broken steel sheets to structure curvy, repetitive forms with refined rusty surfaces. They carry out a feel of antiquity, reminiscent of the weathered relics dated back to the remote past.

Biography

Born in Tokyo in 1961

Completed Tokyo National University of Fine Arts and Music, Master of Fine Arts

Completed Tokyo National University of Fine Arts and Music, Doctor of Fine Arts

Lived in London from 1997 to 2001

Currently lives in Tokyo

Solo Exhibition

2014   Garelie H, Tokyo, Japan

2013   COEXSIST-Tokyo, Tokyo, Japan

2008   Akiyama Gallery, Tokyo, Japan

Atagoyama Art Works, Tokyo, Japan

2007   Yokohama Portside Gallery, Yokohama, Japan

Hongo Shin Memorial Museum of Sculpture, Sapporo, Japan

Group Exhibition

2009   "Water and Land" Nigata Art Festival, Nigata City, Japan

2007   The 40th Anniversary of Japanese Government Overseas Study Program for Artist, Agency for Cultural Affairs, Tokyo, Japan

創作理念

　　作品對我來說或許就像是空氣一樣的存在。說是「空氣」，也是在包含了色調或者是重量感等各式各樣的要素之下才會成立、才可以感受得到，而感受的方法也因人而異，就像時代與季節的變化一樣。

　　只是，最重要的是，我存活在當下的時代之中，在這個季節裡，存活在高雄這個地方，從所感受到的空氣衍生出我的作品。我想這是在其他場域所無法實現的，就算實現了，作品的造型也會有大幅度的差異。

　　平常我在創作雕塑時，心中都會有如在空間中畫素描一般的意識，我絕不會在作品造形之中崁入觀念上的東西。如何維持最初創作的感動與熱情，換言之，就是維持自己與作品之間的關聯，這是一直到創作的最後階段我都不曾放棄的想法，將初衷貫徹執行從來都是我的堅持。

　　這一次，雖然使用的是廢鋼材，我仍是以在空間中畫素描的感覺來進行創作。對於創作特定造型意義的作品，我還是不太能接受，因為我希望能讓眾多的觀眾在欣賞作品時可以自由產生各式各樣的想法。

　　還有，我最後還是避開了上彩，那是因為，我想將廢鋼材的獨特色澤當成色彩來使用，就像繪畫一樣的感覺來進行，而這不是很好嗎？如果這可以實現的話，這種與繪畫不同的造形與色彩的混合，觀賞者應該是可以透過體驗去感受。為了讓更多的觀賞者可以體驗，我將作品中的一個面，大幅度地敞開，以誘導觀眾進入，從作品的中心位置抬頭仰望，希望他們可以比平常更加強烈地感受到天空的色彩。

在未限定任何具體條件的情況之下，我也希望觀眾們透過這件作品可以感受到「風」，就算是一種漠然的氣氛也行，或者，在眾人的記憶中留下某種東西，亦或者，只是色彩也行。這也就再回到了我創作的最初，因為我的作品在一開始時就決定不嵌入固定的意念，以讓觀者可以面對作品、直接感受。作品就像是在音樂廳被演奏的樂曲，它和聽眾兩者之間或許存在著某種相通之處。作曲家與樂團，還有觀眾，在這樣的關係之下，被限定的鑑賞方式相信是不存在的，下了限制又能怎樣呢？然而，即便如此，應該會有許多人在觀賞過我的作品之後會抱持著這究竟是在表現什麼這樣的疑問，所以，接下來我將試著進行解說。

例如，有這樣的觀賞案例也不錯：

「大地非常的乾燥，然後，在水分與養分皆無的乾涸大地向下紮根的植物，頑強地朝天生長。終於，長出了繁茂的樹葉並且開始開花，而這個造形在某種程度上和人在膜拜時雙手的造形又有幾分相似。總之，這件雕塑也許是祈禱的造形。」

但是，這——終究只是一個例子。

深切的期待這件作品可以永遠地存在於高雄的土地上，被許許多多的民眾所喜愛，並持續傳達永遠不變的訊息。

Creation Motive

Art to me is a vital element, just as air is to human. Elements such as the hue and the weight affect the way people connect with artworks; just like how seasons and times influence people's emotions.

The time I live in, the season surrounding me, and the land of the city I am stepping on at this moment, have all contributed to my creation. The surrounding of the artist is the most important element in the process of creating. I couldn't have accomplished the same piece of artwork elsewhere. Even if I had tried, the outline of the artwork would be distinct.

Usually when I create a piece of sculpture, I would only draw a sketch in my mind. Never would I impose any stereotype on my creations. The inspiration originated from the bottom of my heart is the most precious quality that I possess during the process of creating. Maintaining connections with my creations is something I have been insisting on doing.

This time, despite that the materials provided were recycled steel, I still pictured the contours of my artwork in my mind before I started on my creation. As I mentioned before, I prefer creating artworks that allow people to experience direct connection with them. Creating artworks under the restriction of styles or forms does not suit me.

I didn't paint my sculpture in the end, because the unique hue of steel is already a special kind of paint itself. Wouldn't it be nice to present the original characteristic of the material to the visitors? Creating a sculpture from steel is different from painting, I hope the visitors can appreciate the differences between the two styles of art. In order to achieve that, I created a wide open on one side of the sculpture to invite visitors in to look up the sky from the center of

the sculpture. I hope they can appreciate the shades of the sky in a different way.

Not being limited to any titles or forms, I hope the visitors can feel something through this sculpture: the serene atmosphere, a whiff of wind, or even a memorable and colorful moment in the past. This is my original intention. I want to invite the visitors to experience a direct connection with the artwork without any stereotypes or assumptions. An artwork is like a piece of music being performed in a concert hall, it connects with the audience in its own way. The graceful relationship between the composer, the band and the audience exists because art is not an object that can be restricted to any form or description. What is the meaning of giving any

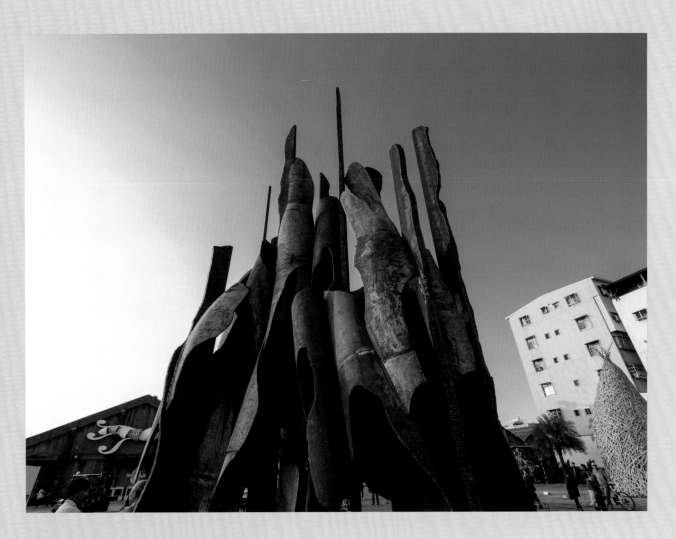

artwork a title? Nevertheless, I assume many visitors might still be confused and would like to know my perspective. I would try to explain my creation motive in the following passage.

Might just as well picture this: "The towering plant put its roots down in the dry land without water or nutrition, it grows indomitably as it stretches upward into the sky. Finally, the plant flourishes and blossoms bloom. The outline, to some degree, looks like a person holding his/her hands together praying. In conclusion, the contours of the sculpture may be the posture of a person praying."

I hope profoundly that this sculpture will be displayed in Kaohsiung forever and that it would inspire those who come to see it.

尚曉風
Shang, Xiao-Feng

作品：海之夢
Dreams of Ocean

　　尚曉風畢業於北京的中央美院，赴澳洲進修與創作多年之後，輾轉回到他的母校任教，並多次參與重要的雕塑展出。身為科班養成的藝術家又兼具雕塑教師的雙重身份，讓尚曉風對雕塑本體的探討與雕塑傳統的創新，別具使命感。他批判中國當代藝術的功利主義現象，標舉藝術之形而上層面的精神價值，以「為藝術而藝術」為創作信念。旅居澳洲期間的抽象雕塑實驗，引領尚曉風形塑自我觀看雕塑的不同視角。他跳脫視覺再現，遊走於抽象與具像之間，不僅回歸純粹的造型實驗，也投入材料、過程、觀念的綜合探索，力圖革新雕塑語言。

簡歷

中央美術學院雕塑系並獲文學學士學位
澳大利亞墨爾本大學碩士學位
中央美院雕塑系教授、碩士生導師、四工作室主任

展覽

2013	CAFA 教師作品展，CAFA 畫廊
2013	中國雕塑年鑒展－國家大劇院
2011	中國姿態－第二屆中國雕塑大展
2011	國家大劇院雕塑邀請展，北京
2011	開悟－大同國際雕塑雙年展，大同
2011	中・韓現代雕刻展，北京
2011	中國雕塑年鑒展，北京
2009	《還鄉》藝術展，北京 798 林大畫廊
2008	798 紅三房畫廊，北京
2007	中央美院通道畫廊，北京
2006	中央美院通道畫廊，北京
1994	維多利亞藝術學院畫廊，墨爾本
1992	鮑威爾街畫廊，墨爾本

Shang Xiao-Feng

pursued his studies in Australia and stayed there for his creation for years after he completed his training from the Central Academy of Fine Arts in Beijing. Later he returned to CAFA as a teacher and exhibited in many significant sculpture events. Academically trained and teaching in an academic institute, Shang has a great sense of mission in exploring the tradition and new development of sculpture. While criticizing the inclination to utilitarianism in the contemporary Chinese art society, Shang eagerly advocates the metaphysical value of art and the ideal of "art for art's sake". During his stay in Australia, Shang's experiments on the creation of abstract sculpture has led him to look into sculpture from different angles. Thus he broke away from simply considering visuality and worked between abstract and figurative art as his approach to pure forms, materials, manufacture procedures as well as art concepts in order to reform sculptural language.

Biography

Bachelor degree at China Central Academy of Fine Arts
Master's Degree at University of Melbourne
Professor of China Central Academy of Fine Arts

Exhibitions

2013	"CAFA Teacher's Exhibition", Gallery CAFA
2013	"Chinese Sculpture Almanac Exhibition", National Theater, China
2011	"Chinese posture - 2nd China Sculpture Exhibition"
2011	"National Theater Sculpture Invitational Exhibition", Beijing
2011	"Enlightenment - Datong International Sculpture Biennale", Datong, China
2011	"China-Korea Modern Sculpture Exhibition", Beijing
2011	"Chinese Sculpture Almanac Exhibition",Beijing
2009	"Coming Home" Art Exhibition, Linda Gallery, Beijing
2008	Loft 3 Gallery, Beijing
2007	Art Gallery of China Central Academy of Fine Arts
2006	Art Gallery of China Central Academy of Fine Arts
1994	Art Gallery of Victorian College of the Arts, Melbourne
1992	Powell St. Gallery, Melbourne

創作理念

　　《海之夢》的創作過程基本是一個即興的創作過程，在來到臺灣高雄之前，我沒有做構思和構圖方面的工作，沒有做草稿的準備，而是把自己的思考放在即將面對的材料之想象。因為不知道將要面對的材料（回收廢棄鋼材）的狀態，所以也就無法做具體的設想。真正的思考是在看到了東和鋼鐵材料現場開始，當進入材料現場那一刻，我即開始了與材料的溝通。我將我感興趣的材料做了記號，頭腦中開始萌現出作品的原始形態，我要將這種感覺轉化為雕塑空間。

　　我在東鋼料廠所選的大多是彎曲的 H 鋼和厚鋼板，它們大多數是建築橋樑和大型工程機械部件，它們有著輝煌的過去，支撐過巨大重力，在回收的過程中又被無比巨大的力量所扭曲，在它上面感受到能量傳達，而這正是我工作的最重要元素。

　　回到工作場地之後，我面對自己選定的廢舊鋼材做進一步的審視，企圖搞清楚他們吸引我的能量是由何而來，這將是我新作品的靈魂。我開始思考和構圖，造形，空間安排等等。首先要解決雕塑與地面如何接觸，由於本次藝術節的組織者高雄市文化局對作品的高度有明確的要求，不能低於 5 米，這件作品就要從地面向空中發展。而我不想自己的作品「長腿」即結構上的支撐被視為造形的一部分。所以一開始很糾結，找不到雕塑與地面接觸的方式，以及向空中發展的契機。幸運的是，我發現了材料中有能夠組成圓盤的鋼板，而且是非常完美的圓形狀態，這使我興奮不已。因為這個核心元素讓我能夠向空中發展並同時確立了雕塑與地面的接觸方式。接下來我就做了基本的草圖，這件作品大致的結構和型態就有了。

　　它的造形是由三個基本元素組成，基座部分是彎曲的 S 形，與地面穩定接觸，同時產生一種蠕動的感覺。中間是一個完整的圓形像一個立起來的飛盤，又像某種海貝殼的形狀，並產生一種滾動的感覺。上面是部分扭曲的 H 鋼組成，飛向空中的夢幻圖形，即像雲又像某種海洋生物。我希望我的作品不是完全抽象的，它也有某種具象的暗示和象征性，也希望人們在我的作品中能找到心性的共鳴。

　　由於我所選擇的材料比較厚，所以後期工作需要很多即興的安排和處理，花費了大量時間在材料的空間造形連接上。整個工作過程雖然艱辛但卻很快樂，因為它充滿了未知和驚喜。我把它叫做《海之夢》，作為我為高雄這個美麗的海港城市創作的第一件作品，寄予了對高雄的美好祝願，留在臺灣，並存於我心！

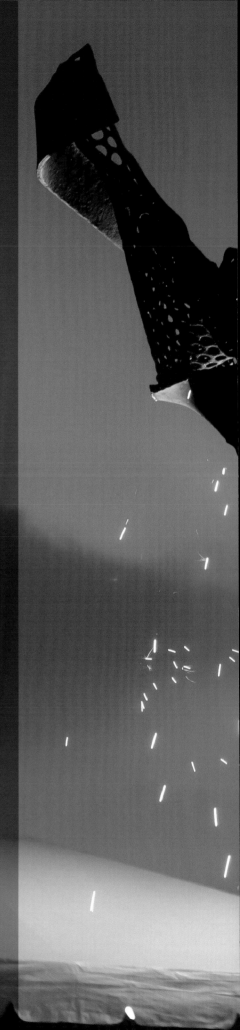

Creation Motive

Dreams of Ocean was an improvisation. Before I arrived in Kaohsiung, I hadn't given any thought to how I would compose it. Instead of drafting, I tried to let my imagination flow within the materials. However, because I hadn't seen the forms of the materials(recycled steel) at that time, nothing concrete was pictured in my head. The moment I really started to feel the materials with my heart was the moment I saw those recycled steel on site. I put marks on the pieces of materials I was interested in. Vague contours then emerged in my head, urging me to transform the inspiration into sculptures.

The materials I picked were mostly twisted H beams and thick steel from bridges and large machines. Before they were extruded with enormous weight, they had been used to support extremely heavy objects. I could feel this splendid transference of energy within the recycled steel, which was demonstrated as the main spirit of my artwork later on.

After I went back to my work place, I observed carefully the scrap that I have selected, trying to find out where the energy that attracted me so much had come from, as this inspiration would be the soul of my artwork. I worked on various dimensions such as the style, the spatial arrangement and the composition of the sculpture. The first problem that needed to be solved was how to create an artwork standing from the ground and stretching upward for over 5 meters, because the Bureau of Cultural Affairs of Kaohsiung City Government, the host team of this year's art festival, had specified that all sculptures should be at least 5 meters tall. I didn't want my artwork to "grow legs", meaning I didn't want the supportive structure to be seen as a part of the design. This troubled me for a while because I couldn't figure out an appropriate way that would ensure my sculpture standing on the ground and stretching upward. Fortunately, I discovered there were steel plates which could be welded into a perfectly rounded shape. I was excited over this idea, because creating an artwork stretching way up from the ground turned out to be doable. Thereupon I blocked in the structure and the contours of my sculpture.

The outline of my sculpture consists of three main parts. The S-shaped podium was laid down on the ground, creating a stable yet wriggly image. The middle part is a full circle which looks like a standing frisbee or some features of sea shells floating in the sea waves. The upper part was made from partially twisted H beams. The up-stretched circle may be clouds or creatures. I hope my artwork is not too abstract for the public and that the implications and symbolism are well conveyed. I also hope that anyone who came could share my feelings.

Due to the fact that the materials I had chosen were thick, I spent a great amount of time on joining separate parts of the materials together. The whole creation process was arduous but pleasant, because I had no idea what would happen the next moment, as if I was on an adventure. I named my sculpture Dreams of Oceans. As my first piece of artwork created for Kaohsiung, I wish all the best to this beautiful harbor city. Dreams of Oceans shall stay in Taiwan, but it will always live in my heart!

劉柏村
Liu, Po-Chun

作品：雲端漫步
Roaming over Clouds

藝術家劉柏村先是在臺灣藝專繼而至巴黎高等美院完成他的專業養成教育，早年曾嘗試不同媒材，後漸專注於鋼鐵雕塑創作。他曾擔任東和鋼鐵廠駐廠藝術家，並受邀參加國內外重要特展，以及匈牙利、韓國、日本、中國等各大雕塑創作營。他的藝術成就屢獲獎項肯定，包括中山文藝獎與吳三連文藝獎兩項殊榮。線與面交錯組成的有機造型、與環境場域的呼應，是劉柏村作品的特色。他多以人物與植物為題，使用表面鏽蝕的鋼鐵為材料，對工業化為世界帶來的改變，包括它對自然生態、人工環境、人類勞動情形的影響，提出回應與反思。

簡歷

法國國立巴黎高等藝術學院雕塑系碩士
國立臺灣藝術大學雕塑系教授迄

個展

2013　東和鋼鐵企業苗栗廠駐廠作品發表會
2012　淡水微笑莊園《鋼鐵化身 II》
2012　韓國首爾皇家畫廊個展《金剛變身》
2011　國立臺灣藝術大學文創園區畫廊個展《鋼鐵化身》
2011　朱銘美術館韓國成東勳－臺灣劉柏村雙個展《金英雄・破神話》

聯展

2014　韓國釜山雙年專題展
2013　福爾摩沙雕塑雙年展於高雄
2013　日本太田原市博物館展
2013　第二屆中國青島國際雕塑藝術節大展
2013　《力量，美在哪裡？》韓國首爾奧林匹克雕塑公園 SOMA 美術館二十五周年專題特展
2012　臺灣雙年展於臺中國家美術館

Liu Po-Chun

completed his professional education in the National Taiwan University of Arts(former National Taiwan Academy of Arts) and the École Supérieure Libre d'art de Paris. He had experimented on various materials before focusing on iron and steel. Liu was the artist-in-residence in the Tung Ho Steel factory and has been invited to exhibit and work at sculpture workshops in Hungary, Korea, Japan and China. Liu has received many art prizes, including the Sun Yat-Sen Culture Foudation's Literary and Art Creation Prize and Wu San-Lian Art Award. Liu's art responds to the milieu with interlaced and organic forms of lines and planes, he represents human figures or plants with rusted and itched steel to reflect the impacts to natural ecology, man-made environment and labor conditions brought by industrialization.

Biography

Master of Fine Arts in Sculpture, École Nationale Supérieure des Beaux-Arts de Paris
Professor at Department of Sculpture, National Taiwan University of Arts

Exhibitions

2013   Tung-Ho Steel Artist-in-resident program Exhibition

2012   "Embodiment of Steel II", Smiley Mansion, Tamsui

2012   Solo Exhibition at Royal Gallery, Seoul

2011   Solo Exhibition at Cultural Creative Industry Cooperation Park, National Taiwan University of Arts

2011   Joint Exhibition with Dong-Hun Sung at Juming Museum

Group Exhibition

2014   Busan Biennale

2013   Formosa Sculpture Biennale in Kaohsiung

2013   Exhibition at Otawara Museum, Japan

2013   2nd International Sculpture Art Festival in Qingdao, China

2013   SOMA museum 25th Anniversary Exhibition, Seoul

2012   Taiwan Biennial at National Taiwan Museum of Fine Arts

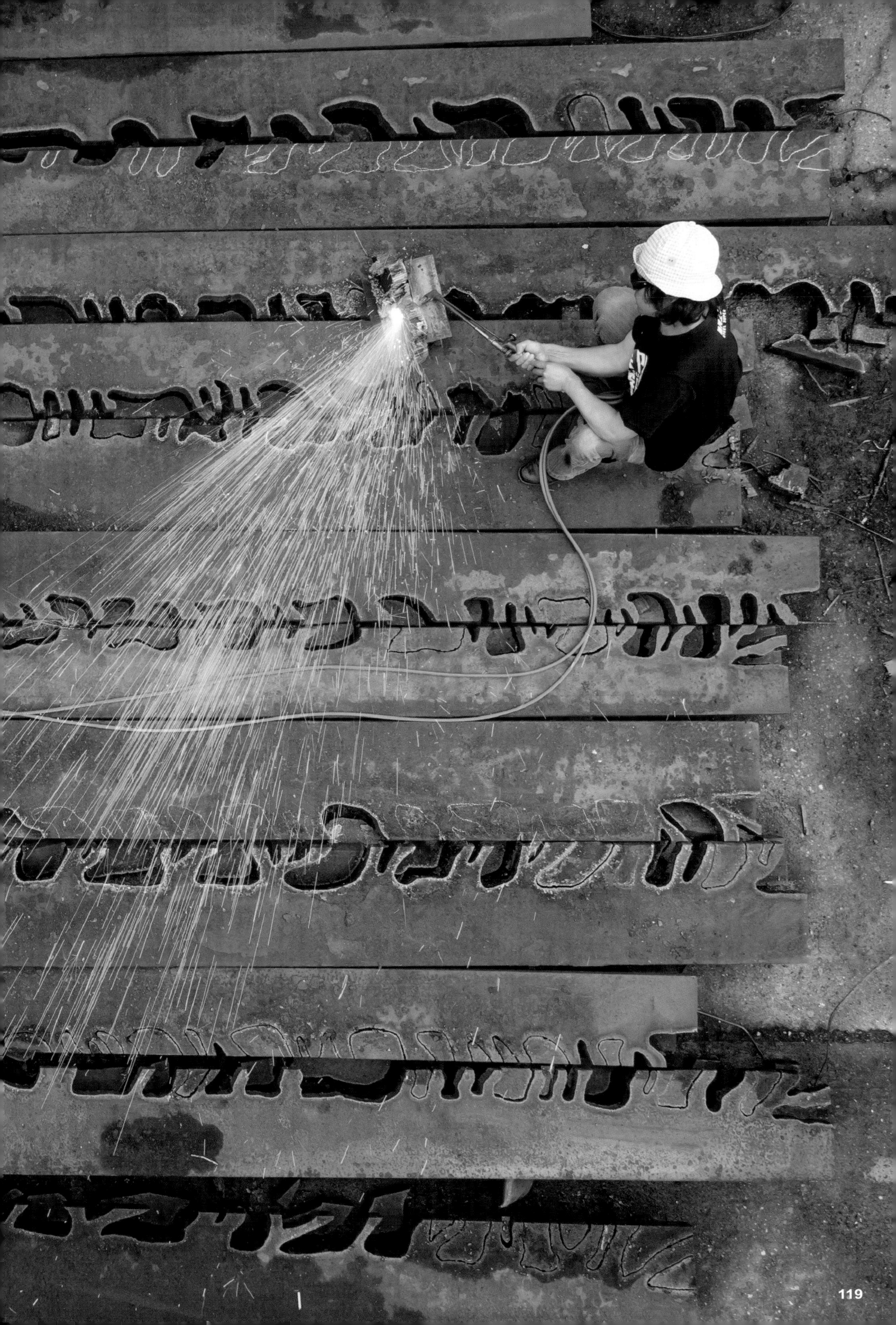

創作理念

　　曾經在東和鋼鐵苗栗廠區駐廠創作過兩次，對這一片廠區的鋼鐵場景，已經是相當熟悉。只是如何從中選取材料與表現，來回應高雄國際鋼雕藝術節「無限上鋼」的主題，同時又能銜接個人創作的延續性，這是我一直不斷思考的問題。當然，也由於廠區僅能提供廢棄的現成物鋼材，因此藝術家們的所能選擇的材料，自然也導向被設定的某種扭曲不規則且具強烈語彙的物件型態。另外每位藝術家在這短短的兩個多禮拜期間有 20 噸鋼材可運用，如何拉出藝術家彼此創作之間的差異，同時展現鋼鐵的更大的可能性與能量，也必得要考量。同時永久設置場所乃為高雄駁二特區周圍高樓大廈林立的景點，如何連接自然與文化，亦成為我一開始切入的思考點。

　　在工業機械年代裡，科技快速發展，生產條件改變，使得機械複製之「量化」語言，成為這個時代必然的生活表徵。尤其身處在現代都會，大廈林立的文明環境裡，一種理性而僅見垂直斷截面的鋼構叢林，遮蔽了大地水平景緻的視野，在快速升降梯的高度轉變與震盪衝擊下，導致對本原內在價值和意義的疏離。使得我們玄妙的感官知覺意識，對於自然和空間的想像和視野，慢慢退化萎縮。我們是否再也無力認識真實的世界、感知事物真正的位置、狀態、現象和姿勢？我們的認知是否一直因而困惑、只見規則卻無能有指示？

　　依此的理解，現代文明中所衍生了一些複雜的情境，強顯了事物本質是建立於環境之內，物質性存在也無間斷地改變，個人主觀與聚合的潛在意識皆從屬於環境機制的歷史客觀性。而對於個人來說，在藝術創造的自我世界建構中，生活也成為我創作的取材內容。因此如何去探究這些工業材料以轉化出時代之精神？如何展現生產的生態機制和藝術

與現實共生的美學？如何經過材料的認知，以表達出個人所欲傳達的語言？如何去透過這些工業性材料在當代藝術中進一步開拓具延展性的語言？

　　此次的創作，希冀著墨於此種複雜情境的改變，企圖探求反應人類身體與現代工業環境所產生的根本矛盾現象。所以在作品實踐過程中，試圖從解構的意象美學，從表現的過程中所凝結的觸視張力擴展開來，期望再進一層探討工業、人本及自然之關係。此次的作品，個人以單純形式回應複雜的情境，在此只選擇了樹形與雲朵兩個符號，同時利用工業大量生產之複製的長條平面鋼板與地金之有機性質為主要材料，藉由剪影的手法，運用工業性火焰強大的切割力量，作為造形表現運作的切入點。首先，地面是由大小不同的鋼材雲朵符號所鋪成，以構成長條型的雲端步道。接下來，依此步道分隔排列，豎立起一群猶如高山中參天古木之姿的長條式平板樹形，同時將樹形由中間直線裁切分開為兩半，進而拉出相對空間，形成人身可穿梭的入口。然後，在這規格化之堅硬鋼材的垂直樹形頂端，運用片狀地金的有機物質性，如地形圖般的由外而內切割出似雲朵般的輪廓線條，進而與之平行環扣、交織構成，同時因其形態透空的穿透性，做為作品連結天地的介層，也讓元素與空間產生全面性融入的互動關係。

　　因此，藉此自然符號的詮釋，以及其層疊的堆積中，使得作品整體乍看之下如素描或山水圖畫般的自然叢林景象，但也由於材料之工業性質，同時翻轉出一種人化自然中之真實空間的再現探索，或說是一種幻象式、虛擬般的變異場景，但這也是一種個人主觀情境思維中的空間領域，以期召喚引導觀者漫遊走入於正值建構狀態的「雲端現場」。也由於觀者進入作品的參與互動，在移動觀看作品的同時，也成為作品被觀看的元素之一。　進而地使得作品藉由此種凝聚性的特定場域，由內而外地，激發作品潛在的力量，延伸擴展至整個空間環境，以建構一種透過藝術家所量身定做的當代工業性之社會環境及人文背景的「人化自然的美學現場」。

Creation Motive

I have already created artworks at Miao Li Works of Tung Ho Steel Enterprise for two times previously, so I'm familiar with the steel material area. However, how to pick the suitable material for creating a piece of sculpture of which the topic is in accordance with that of Kaohsiung International Steel and Art Festival-- Steel Super, and demonstrating my personal style at the same time have been the problem that have kept me thinking. Due to the fact that the material provided by Tung Ho was steel, there was a certain extent of restriction in terms of forms. The twisted, irregular and strong nature of steel should be displayed more or less in the sculpture. In addition, during the short period of two to three weeks, every artist had 20 tons of steel available. How to distinguish one artist's style from another and display the beauty of strength and the energy within steel also needed to be considered. Sculptures would be displayed permanently at scenic spots within the tall modern buildings around The Pier-2 Art Center. How to create a sculpture that can connect with the nature and the culture was also an important aspect that had kept me thinking.

In the age of industry and machines, technology has developed rapidly, conditions of manufacturing has changed and the importance of quantity has increased, contributing to the characteristics of this industrial age. Living in a modern city with those tall, rational and vertical steel buildings blocking the scenic view, the inner value of human has retrograded as if it was torn as the elevator go up or down.

The delicate human consciousness and the imagination toward the nature and space have fallen back for the same reason. Will human be incapable of feeling the true world we exist in ever since? Will human's consciousness be confused and restricted to the forms of the buildings?

 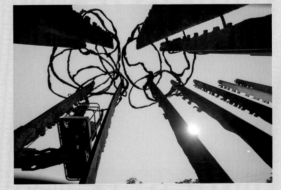

Accordingly, human nature has changed as our community develop. This points out that the nature of a substance depends on the environment. As time goes on and as the form of material existence change, subjectivity and the subconscious mind of human have both been subject to the environmental system. During the creating process, artists build heir ideal world. Their life experiences bring out inspirations. How to explore the souls of these industrial materials that have been transformed from one age to another? How to present the combination of the ecosystem and industrial production, the harmony between art and reality? How to fully express one's own words through the relation with materials? How to put a step forward to enrich contemporary art through those industrial materials?

The main idea of this sculpture is to present the changes of the complicated states of mind. It aims at discovering the contradiction of human's mind and the modern industrial environment. During the process of creation, I attempted to analyze the relation between the industry, human and the nature through decomposing the esthetic composition of the artwork, and also through expanding the visual tension from within. In this sculpture, I created objects of simple forms for responding to the complex environment. The symbols I have chosen were trees and clouds. Meanwhile, I used many bars of steel produced through industrialized mass production procedure and chunks of iron residue to create the sculpture. The silhouetted image forged by ferocious fire is the main characteristic of the sculpture. Steel clouds of different sizes paving the ground make a long trail in clouds. Silhouetted cluster of tall trees standing over it are cut into two parts from the center, creating an entrance with enough space for us to pass. At the top of these vertical silhouetted tree shapes of steel, the irregular curved lines of clouds are cut from chunks of iron residues from the outside. These two parts of the sculpture are parallel yet linked, allowing the invisible elements in the air interact through the hollow vertical objects as well as composing a medium between the sky and the ground.

The piled up display of signified nature make the sculpture seem like a piece of sketch or a scenery painting at first appearance. However, the sculpture is endued with a deeper meaning because of the industrial materials used in the creation. The sculpture can be seen as an imagination, a fictitious transformation scene, or any image related to the viewer's personal experience. The sculptor invites visitors to roam over clouds on site. Visitors can experience a direct connection with the sculpture by actively moving within, which is also an important element of the display. The potential energy of the sculpture can be fully fired up as visitors gather at the scene. It flows within the space, building a "personified esthetics scene", with the industrial background and human civilization combined through the hands of the sculptor.

梁任宏

作品：**What is 花枝**
What is a Cuttlefish

Liang, Jen-Hung

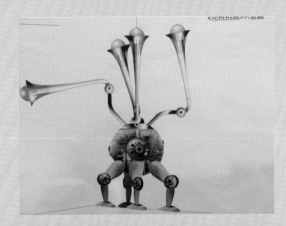

　　出生也定居於南臺灣的梁任宏，早先曾嘗試不同的工作，後才輾轉專職投入藝術創作。大型的動態藝術是梁任宏最具代表性的創作路線，他或以塑膠、壓克力，或以金屬等不同的材料完成的雕塑，時而依賴自然界的風吹與水流，時而搭配機械動力、雷射、電子攝影等等現代媒材，在環境中展現動力、光線或聲響等複合效果的創作，微妙地結合機械秩序與自然韻律。他的作品曾獲得南北兩都的美術大獎肯定，不斷受邀參與許多重要展覽以及公共藝術創作。知名導演黃明川曾透過鏡頭追溯梁任宏獨特的創作歷程，以「動人的南方傳奇」為其下註解。

簡歷
臺南藝術學院造型藝術研究所
雕塑藝術創作者

展覽
2013 《球》，高雄國際鋼雕藝術節，高雄
2012 《歸魚》，臺灣林邊車站公共藝術，屏東
2010 《也通風也報信》，臺北捷運 R4 車站公共藝術，臺北市
2009 《上街頭》，臺北當代藝術館地下室實驗創意秀場，臺北市
2008 《太極風》，朱銘美術館，臺北
2008 《時光隧道》，臺灣燈會，臺南
2007 《機械總動員》，高雄市立美術館，高雄
2006 《捕風捉影》、《方桌旁的風景》，國際鋼雕藝術節，高雄
2005 《說白話》，當代藝術館，臺北市
2004 《巴斯卡在高雄》，國際鋼雕藝術節，高雄
2003 《Shoebox-Story》，夏威夷大學美術館首展，美國
2002 《高雄的景觀窗：存在的儀式 1》，臺北新聞文化中心，巴黎
2001 《國際貨櫃藝術節：前進撒哈拉》，高雄海洋之星，高雄

Liang Jen-Hung

was born in Tainan and currently lives in Tainan. Having tried various jobs, Liang finally decided to devote himself to art. He took the path of kinetic art and applies plastic, acrylic or metal among other materials in his sculpture. Liang's sculpture can be activated by wind gusts or water flows, and some of them are coupled with mechanically or electrically powered media, such as laser or digital photography. Liang combines kineticism, light and sounds to produce compound effects of the sophisticated mechanic orders as well as subtle natural rhymes. Liang's artworks have been awarded major art prizes given by both the southern and northern capitals of Taiwan and exhibited in many significant events, including several public art projects. Notable film director Huang Ming-Chuan has recorded Liang's unique way of creation and credited him as "a touching legend from southern Taiwan".

Biography

Graduated from Tainan National University of the Arts, Graduate Institute of Plastic Arts
Currently works as a professional sculptural artist

Exhibitions

2013   "Ball", Kaohsiung International Steel & Iron Sculpture Festival
2012   "Home-Coming Fish", Public Art for Linbian train station, Pin-tong
2010   "To communicate", Public Art for Metro, Taipei
2009   "Go to the Streets" Basement for Experimental Creativity, Museum of Contemporary Art, Taipei
2008   "Way of Tai Chi", Juming Museum, Taipei
2008   "Time Tunnel", Lantern Festival, Tainan
2007   "All Machines" Kaohsiung Museum of Fine Arts
2006   "Chase the Wind and Clutch at Shadows, View from the Side-Table", Kaohsiung International Steel & Iron Sculpture Festival
2005   "Talk Colloquial", Kaohsiung International Steel & Iron Sculpture Festival
2004   "Pascal in Kaohsiung", Kaohsiung International Steel & Iron Sculpture Festival
2003   "Shoebox-Story", Art Museum of University of Hawaii
2002   "Viewfinder of Kaohsiung: Ceremony of Existence 1", Centre Cultural de Taiwan à Paris
2001   "To Sahara", Kaohsiung International Container Arts Festival

創作理念

　　自然環境提供物種演化的元素，工業環境提供人工智能進階的基礎，仿生科技模糊了物種的出處，自然演化以退化作為進化的手段，仿生科技卻以進階取代人類逐漸退化的本能，當人類的能力逐漸被替代，人工智能與自然演化聯姻，接管了演化世界，奇異的物種豐富了失能的人類世界。我可愛嗎？人類！

　　「鐵」這個元素，曾經讓人類以工業文明之名，雄霸了現代！現代之後「鐵」的重要性，似乎不再那麼絕對，但是其特質仍然無可取代，「鐵」好似自然與人工間的蟲洞，搓揉、打造、還原，都在一念之間，「鐵」在自然與人工之間遊走，並給雙方帶來信息，往來頻繁的「鐵」累積並豐富了他自己的生命，他說：我有我的感情，我有我的道德感，我想選擇我存在的形式，假人類藝術創作之名，打造我吧！

　　用人工打造，把我送入風中，四肢隨著環境的流態伸展，我成了人工與自然之間的臨時介面，這是我此時此刻的選擇，What is 花枝？誒！名字有那麼重要嗎！

Creation Motive

The nature is a necessary condition for evolution. The industrial environment, on the other hand, facilitates the development of artificial intelligence. Bionic technology has blurred the origin of species and replaced the degenerating human instinct with advanced progresses. Evolution has proceeded with the help of modern technology. As technology has gradually superseded manpower, artificial intelligence has joined forces with evolution, the nature of evolution has changed. Precious species have enriched the disabled human civilization ever since. Am I cute, human?

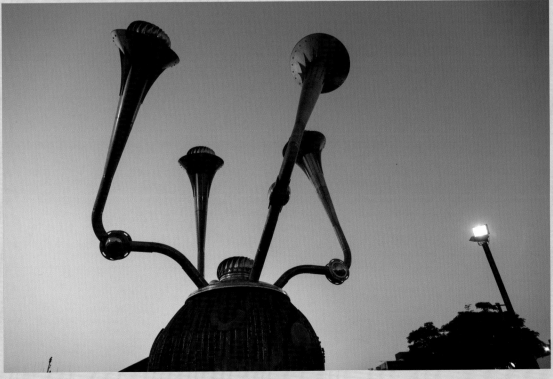

Human once predominated the world by using metal as industrial civilization developed. However, the value of metal as human moved on to the stage of modern civilization. Nevertheless, the characteristics of metal are unique; just like a wormhole connecting the nature and human life. Metal can be squeezed, forged or melted, it shuttles between the nature and human civilization, conveying some kind of message. Metal has been transformed from one shape to another various times in the past, if metal can speak like we do, it might say: I can feel, I have my own morality, I am also a substance in the nature, I can choose which form I want to live in. Include me in your artwork! Forge me!

Forge me, send me into the wind! Let my limbs sway within the flows. Make me the temporary interface of the nature and human. What is a cuttlefish? Is name really that important?

技術團隊
About the Tech Team

創作營執行總監｜蔡坤霖
創作營技術統籌｜鄭陽晟
創作營協力廠商｜宇建形象有限公司
Executive Director: Tsai Kun-Lin
Technical Director: Cheng Yang-Cheng
Technical Supplier: Yu-Jian CO., LTD Taiwa

記 2014 高雄國際鋼雕藝術節論壇活動

紀錄與整理：黃慕怡

場次一
藝術家現身說法
時　　間：2015 年 1 月 3 日（星期六）13:30- 16:30
地　　點：高雄駁二藝術特區 大義倉庫，火腿藝廊
主持人：劉俊蘭
與談人：Riccardo Cardero、Nicolay Polissky、
　　　　前田哲明、尚曉風、梁任宏、劉柏村

主持人：與過去相較，遼闊的創作基地、豐富的材料、國際化的參與，都是這屆國際鋼雕藝術節「無限上鋼」的獨特之處。參與的六位藝術家，將逐一跟我們分享他們個人的藝術創作。

Riccardo Cardero：很高興能為大家介紹我的藝術創作生涯。首先1960 年代我將小碎片放大成石膏來探索動感，也反映當時義大利藝術表現主義階段。我的工作模式相當傳統，是先有模型再將尺寸放大成作品。1964 年後材料轉為聚脂加色彩，主題為 1960 年代流行文化，如足球員或太空人。1968 年完成生涯中第一件在國外展出之作，塑料有鋼鐵色澤質感，逐漸去除基座，用懸吊加強記念性；這時也進入幾何階段，採用三角、方型來對話，創造空間感。1976 年採用「窗戶」或「門」的元素，將外在風景放進雕塑，讓堅硬的結構體加上植物般的柔軟線條。1978-79年以自然主題之作參加威尼斯雙年展，此時杜林流行「貧窮藝術」，我卻在構成與尺寸上與之背道而馳，追尋內心自我。後來我嘗試做出「裸女」主題，再回到「景物」，結合陶瓷、鐵與鋼鐵。我近年發展大尺寸作品，其中「圓形」最具律動感而成為我的創作主軸。

Nicolay Polissky：我在蘇維埃嚴峻的氣氛下成長，直到蘇維埃 1997年解體，長達二十年的思想鉗制對我的藝術影響很大。我四十二歲時為了改變而返回鄉下 Nikola Lenivets，在那裡做一系列的雪人，春天時用乾草做古祭壇，秋天用收割好的乾草、嚴冬用生火的木柴，堆疊加上燈光與煙霧，產生壯麗的視覺效果。

我的概念是用藤蔓與樹枝在鄉下做當地沒有的現代化造形，像是類似巴黎鐵塔的《電視塔》；我在塔上放了蔬果種子，兩年半後舉辦豐收季；俄國重要節慶「謝肉節」來臨，燃燒作品歡慶冬去春來，還邀請藝人表演慶祝。另外十六公尺高的《燈塔》在河畔以枯枝來完成。不同於已燒掉的《電視塔》，這件作品還在 Nikola Lenivets 當地至今天已存十年。對我來說，作品一定要與大自然融合。《火鳥》用鋼鐵製作，加上內部以柴火高溫燃

燒；作品《火山爆發》以藤蔓為材料纏繞，內置燈光來模擬火焰效果。當俄國鄉下挖掘出兩三千年前的考古遺跡，我在那做了最大的作品，像教堂或馬雅廟宇，是對宇宙的思考。另外我在法國的創作，因為考量當地葡萄酒有盛名，所以用葡萄藤做成大型建築，靈感來自巴黎龐畢度中心的水管構造。

前田哲明：我已年屆五十，初作油畫後逐漸踏入雕塑創作領域。70年代新的藝術浪潮開始時，我從東京藝術大學畢業並獲文化廳補助去倫敦。我有幸在約克夏雕塑公園舉辦個展，用耐候鋼、鐵、不鏽鋼網、鋁和壓克力來嘗試材質的趣味性。

2002年倫敦歐魯先教會計劃，起因於2000年教會遭祝融之災，我得知倫敦教會協會要改建成現代風的水泥教會，於是想在裡面展覽。教會信眾希望唱詩席不要拆掉，我發起「復興」而非重建的藝術計劃。為此安全協會進行鑑定，也克服教會組織裡頭的反對勢力等，前後費時兩年。我用無數的PC管指向天際，象徵串聯前世今生，邁向未來等願景。我用簡潔造形，也用被火燻燒過瓦片又加金箔製作。教會照原貌保存下來了，瓦片歸位修復後建築物再生，教會信眾心願得以完成。教會計劃後，我回日本個展，作品將鐵加熱後變形後設置在畫廊，用釣魚線從天花板吊起，呈現風吹搖晃感，是有裝置藝術氛圍的雕塑。此次在高雄現地製作的作品，簡單地用鋼管來作多層次的製作，因氧化程度而有色彩變化。

尚曉風：近十年來我選擇具像人體創作，我獨自生活在工作室內六年，做出五六百件人體塑造。我強調觀念「寫生而不寫實」，或說「做雕塑而不做人體」：人體是工作緣由而不是主題，更不是內容。我只是把人體當成抽象或說「具像形式抽象做」，起頭寫實，做多了就容易達到寫意的狀態。我讓泥性、寫生狀態與我的內在交流，我受抽象表現主義的訓練而又與書法、自然主義結合，這應該是東方藝術家重要的一項特點。我的為自己，而不為公眾創作，即使公共藝術也要與自身有關係才行，這次在駁二的創作也一樣。

梁任宏：剛開始面對我自己，有時旁人會覺得好嚴肅。在那個階段我就像如鐵般重、悶而沉，於是就做出那樣的作品，作品運動也如此重、悶、沉。起初從平面繪畫轉入多媒材而開始思考材質問題，我想表達的是「能量」。我思考動態的問題，我認為生命狀態就是變動的。我覺得整個世界都是一種流態，觀念符合我作品對生命的詮釋，它是不可預期的狀態，美妙的意外。於是我處理流體力學、美妙的機械，形式簡單，卻提供觀眾更多的咀嚼，啟動觀者的微系統。人為了影響生命空間與環境，會對自己不斷地投藥，所以我將膠囊放入環境裡，映照人對自己投藥的行為；人會用對待自己的方式來對待環境。

人類自覺來自開始觀察本來沒有注意到環境細節，如風流的狀態等，在環境中細細咀嚼的事物。關心與思考是必要的，我用不鏽鋼來提供人與環境好而協調的互動關係，用自然的方式、物理的平衡，來聯繫生命的運動。

劉柏村：2004年朱銘美術館邀請展，我突顯「場所」關係而在美術館空間再造一座工業森林。這座森林有八十件鋼樹，設定綠色的光源變化，用單一木幹結構做重複，並安置離心馬達。我使樹木顫抖，還發出了像鳥鳴似的聲音，觀眾觸摸彷彿像觸電。

再提國父紀念館翠亨藝廊的展出。我自己做六頭強壯寫實的玻璃纖維乳牛，五黑一白，表面磨亮到有如汽車烤漆。它們只能在軌道上前後移動，逐步逼近五十元硬幣的大鏡面。放大硬幣上寫了「中華民國兩千年」，當年只是中華民國九十九年，引起了疑問和抗議。另外國父塑像用壓模做成凹陷的負空間，加以藍色的LED光條搖晃，「為什麼國父是凹的？」這一切都可以被解釋。另一重點，有個喇叭可以將牛隻在鐵軌上軌道發出的聲音、觀眾說話地聲音重複播放，呼應國父紀念館流動空間狀態，引發觀眾對錢幣、軌道提問「為什麼？」

從創作營到藝術節：
藝術生產、城市行銷與文化行動

時　間：2015 年 1 月 4 日（星期日）14:00- 16:00
地　點：高雄駁二藝術特區　大義倉庫　火腿藝廊
主持人：劉俊蘭
與談人：張惠蘭、賴永興、劉柏村、梁任宏

主持人：今天有三項討論提綱，第一是「藝術創作營的地方性」，請與會的策展人與藝術家針對地方特色來比較。第二，創作營作為「一種藝術生產方式」，創作型態的挑戰與可能性為何？第三，創作營擴大舉辦為藝術節慶之際，牽涉了藝術推廣與城市行銷，這與藝術本身與文化行動如何並行？是否存在衝突？

橋仔頭糖廠與防空洞藝術節

張惠蘭：我曾多次以藝術家身份參與創作營；而策展人身份則從高雄縣橋仔頭糖廠開始。1999 年底我在橋仔頭糖廠辦活動，2001 年我得到國藝會贊助，正式集結藝術家，串連高雄與台北的藝術資源，藝術節從橋仔頭移到華山藝文中心烏梅酒廠展覽《酸甜酵母菌》。

第一屆的藝術村是「防空洞藝術節」。起初辦了藝術村村長選票活動與工作室開放，藝術家批次進駐小工作室來創作，好奇群眾早晚熱心督促藝術家的製作進展，於是開放工作室參觀交流，結合視覺與表演藝術來介紹「藝術家的一天」。第二屆與第三屆的「防空洞藝術節」，在地形成了陶藝特色，許多藝術家製作藤條，陶藝家以橋仔頭當地材料——糖，來做燻燒，並與其他不同地區、國際的藝術家及民眾交流互動。文化互動的方法包括邀請民眾來橋仔頭遊街、辦理「國際劇場戲劇節」，邀請十八國來串連。回看這年歲已久的記錄，地方型節慶的重點仍在民眾參與與推廣，使創作不僅限是藝術家個人的事。

舉例來說，2001 年日本藝術家使用糖為材料製作傳統日式的桌子與杯盤，邀請觀眾用可樂融化作品。到 2006 年橋仔頭有許多改變，意圖告別舊時代：日本藝術家回顧中國與台灣糖業歷史、台法藝術家就地取材用做鋼鐵焊接、劉丁讚所用糖廠的五分車做成互動藝術品。

主持人：剛才的分享更聚焦人與場所之間的聯繫與問題。在場所方面，藝術家進駐空間並與場域對話，碰觸空間記憶與未知經驗。在人方面，有藝術家間的串連、民眾互動。然而比較高雄鋼雕、苗栗木雕、花蓮石雕，其間差異在於「材料」，這可以說是限制也可說是各地藝術節的特色。

三義木雕的危機與木雕創作營的源起

賴永興：三義木雕創作營至去年（2014 年）已辦理八屆，期間曾中斷兩屆。三義木雕曾經因為發展過度、品質參差不齊，又引進大量大陸創作，使得木雕街上八成木雕產品都是中國製作，還有後繼無人的問題。十年前我參訪時，最年輕的木雕師已經四十幾歲，良好的技術苦無後人肯學習。因此當時找了楊北辰老師來辦理「薪傳營」，讓大專生來傳承。他們學習過程相當辛苦：在酷暑中學生住在民宿，集中工作，每天八點上工、做到下午甚至到晚上。許多學生是大學一年級，全無木雕基礎。藝術家進駐很重要，基層創作營的培育，從工藝朝向藝術發展，逐漸產生影響。能從地方封閉性的創作營發酵，逐步辦理成為國際級的創作營，地方政府值得肯定。

主持人：三義木雕藝術節相當特殊，性質也與花蓮石雕藝術節接近，有推廣和振興地方產業的雙重任務，包含創作營、進駐計畫與木雕聯展。苗栗地區的木雕要從工藝型態轉向藝術性，充滿挑戰。

第五屆鋼雕藝術節回顧

梁任宏：第五屆藝術節名為「鋼鋼好」，指涉精確的創作樣態。金屬創作需要的尺寸準確度比其他材料更高——做木工追求「公分」，但金屬切割尺寸要求「厘米」以下。為了促進交流，我首先使藝術家年齡層拉大，藝術家的類別也擴充邀請了女性藝術家與詩人來參與。2010 年沒有廠商提供材料，這使得藝術家的選擇不受限定，創作樣態因此與其他屆不同。韓國藝術家成東勳的作品《聽樹》在樹上掛鈴，風吹產生音色律動，鄰近居民卻對音響聲感到不滿，作品因此移地，突顯藝術品、環境與民眾的三角關係。另外，女性藝術家黃沛瀅以單純元素——不鏽鋼墊片（washer）來創作、黃筱珊用銅做出精緻作品。而我在倉庫前完成作品《駁浪》，風來會轉動，創作難度來自準確性，而我首次嘗試不在工作室裡完成作品。當時完成的這些作品尺寸也許不是很大，但藝

術家都非常投入，而作品也將永續保存在駁二特區。

設置點的場域概念與藝術生產的創作營

劉柏村：西方創作營透過不同國家區域性的交流來消弭邊界，1997 年達到高潮後就不再這麼強調。一般說來，在西方必會直接告知設置點的場域概念，這種模式使邀請何種藝術家會成為重點。例如我在羅馬尼亞戶外創作營要求自然材料，

當地山區提供長達十幾公尺的大量木頭，就不適合沒有處理原生材料經驗的藝術家。而藝術家改變創作慣性仍要有能力完成作品。

在高雄鋼雕節，藝術家即使有操作能力，卻因尺寸太大，只能選擇指揮而非操作。藝術家仰賴工作團隊，能做超越技能的思考。2012 年的「全民大戀鋼」，我帶藝術家到苗栗鋼鐵廠去看廢鐵，設定了蓬萊倉庫旁的特定展區，藝術家得以在參照中進入創作脈絡。此外，藝

術家間的深刻交流要透過內部座談來完成。

主持人：對興辦機構來說，創作營也是在當前國際經濟危機下有效的小資經濟，在現地、限時、限材之下取得佳作，比起委託製作經濟許多。

張惠蘭：我的思考不太一樣，主要針對建築空間營造、城鄉策略，所以挑選藝術家時，我以藝術網脈考量，首先不會對媒材做出限制。第

二點，我重視藝術家交換的能量。當時橋仔頭所在的高雄縣，政策期待以藝術節慶來整合資源，因此重要的是「串連」。當時配合女性藝術協會的展演而有女性藝術工作坊，與社會政策及與運動應合。

主持人：從地方性思考，藝術節慶在均質與雷同化的全球化時代可能有激進意義，強調地方特質將有如異軍崛起。然而，政治宣傳也可能使藝術理想與文化行動產生矛盾，如某些藝術節僅剩觀光價值。

賴永興：關於藝術節慶的內部可能的矛盾問題，可見於木雕藝術節執行數年後。頒獎典禮像政治家的秀場，但因經費充裕、藝術家進駐、收藏家與觀光客皆成長，整體說來仍相當正面。

劉柏村：創作營本身的產出方式接近表演性質，成品也與城市產生關係。2014年我參加釜山雙年展的創作營，共有三十五位藝術家參與。據說每年有三十萬觀眾以上，當地政府編列預算，視為城市行銷大事，結合地方傳統祭典盛大辦理。從作品來發揚藝術進入生活，生活美學的理念，對於社會教育影響深遠。

梁任宏：我認為工作團隊已經成為高雄市的文化財。因為我有營造、建築的工程經驗，而我創作用工程的概念來完成。我的草根特質可以無隔閡地與技師溝通，其實歷程非常長而複雜，也涉及多類型的創作。日後高雄若要辦理多元材料展覽也可支援。

劉柏村：補充有關城市行銷，去年受邀到韓國有將近二十幾位藝術家，有些國家的隨行記者也全程參加，這是深諳行銷之道的做法。為記者提供交通和住宿費，換得全版的新聞報導，消息能深入社會各階層。

主持人：我想談藝術節慶除了藝術教育、宣傳之外，還有連續舉辦之時的新可能性，都值得思考。即使可能沒有標準答案，帶著思考性的疑問離開也是很好的結束。感謝各位與會。

2014 Kaohsiung International Steel & Iron Art Festival Forum

Written by Huang Mu-Yi

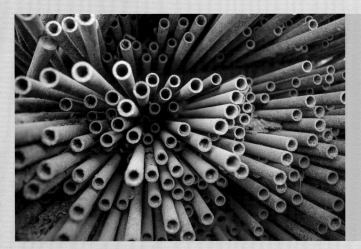

Session One

Meeting the Artists

Time: January 3rd, 2015 (Sat) 13:30-16:30

Venue: HAM Gallery, Da Yi Warehouse,
The Pier 2 Art Center, Kaohsiung

Host: Liu Jun-Lan

Participants: Riccardo Cardero, Nicolay Polissky,
Noriaki Maeda, Shang Xiao-Feng,
Liang Jen-Hung, Liu Po-Chun

Host: Broad working space, abundant materials and international participation are all features that make this year's International Steel & Iron Art Festival-- Steel Super special. Six artists have created artworks for the festival, and now they will share their creative motives with us.

Riccardo Cardero: It's a pleasure to share my experiences in art with you. In the 1960s, I magnified gravels into gypsum to discover the dynamics within, which reflected expressionism in Italy at that time. I have always worked in a traditional way: I make models before producing them into concrete artworks. After 1964, the materials I used changed to polyester with colors as the theme of my artworks was 1960's Popular Culture, such as soccer players or astronauts. In 1968, I created my first piece of artwork displayed overseas. The material I used was plastic with the grayish hue of metal. After I cut the base of the material little by little, I hung the artwork in the air to reinforce its impression on the audience. This was also the beginning of the stage of geometric shapes. Triangles, rectangles

and squares were used to demonstrate extensity. In 1976, elements such as "doors" or "windows" began to appear in my artworks. I carved irregular and curved lines outside the stiff structure in order to demonstrate the beauty of nature through sculptures. From 1978 to 1979, I participated in the Venice Biennial, the artwork that I created used the nature as the theme. Despite the fact that "Arte Povera" was the trend inTorina at that time, I went in the opposite direction in terms of the structure and size of artworks to better understand my inner self. Afterwards, the themes of my artworks went to "nude women" and then went back to "scenery", combining ceramics, metal and steel. I started to create large size artworks in recent years, while "circle" has become the theme of my creations because it is the most dynamic shape. I see the audience as part of my artwork, because their different views can bring out different visual effects and interpretation of the artwork.

Nicolay Polissky: I grew up in an environment with many restrictions under the government of Soviet Union. The Soviet Union didn't fall until 1997, their suppression on thoughts that lasted for 20 years had greatly influenced my creation. I returned to the countryside Nikola Lenivets at the age of 42. I made a series of snowman; I made altar with hay in spring;

I stacked the hay reaped in autumn and the woods used to burn fire in cool winters. Along with lights and smog, I demonstrated magnificent visual effects.

The concept was to create an artwork with vines and branches with modern outlines that didn't exist in the countryside. Take TV Tower for example, this was a piece of artwork that looked similar to the Eiffel Tower. I put seeds of vegetables and fruits on the tower, and celebrated the harvest season two and a half years later. At the Russian Maslenitsa festival, the artwork was burnt to celebrate the end of winter and greet the coming of spring. Some artists were invited to perform at the festival as well. Another piece of artwork The Lighthouse stands 16 meters tall. It was made from dead branches near the riverside. Different from TV Tower, this artwork has stood in Nikola Lenivets for ten years so far. In my opinion, artworks should always be in connection with the nature. Phoenix, another artwork of mine, was made from metal with woods burning inside. As for the artwork Volcanic Eruption, I entwined vines on the outside, with lights inserted inside to create the image of flames. When the historical remains from two to three thousand years ago were discovered in the countryside in Russia, I created the largest piece of artwork there in response to the universe. The contours of this artwork

looked like a church or Mayan temple. Furthermore, considering the good reputation of wine in France, I created a huge building from grape vines when I was there. My inspiration came from the exterior heating and cooling systems of the Pompidou Center.

Noriaki Maeda: I'm nearly 50 years old. After some success in oil painting, I started entering the field of sculpting. In the 1970s while the new trend of art emerged, I graduated from Tokyo National University of Fine Arts and Music and then I went to London on scholarship awarded by the Japanese Cultural Ministry. I had the honor to hold a solo exhibition at Yorkshire Sculpture Park before. During the process of creation, I had fun using corten steel, metal, stainless steel net, aluminum and acrylic.

I took part in the project at All Saints Church in London Dulwich in 2002. The project was carried out because a fire had burnt down the church. When I knew that All Saints Church planned to rebuild the church into a modern cement building, I wanted to hold an exhibition in there. The believers wanted to keep the choir loft in the building, so I initiated a "renaissance art project" instead of "rebuilding" the church. For this reason, it took me two years in total to pass the inspection carried out by security authorities and settle objections within the church. I placed numerous polycarbonate tubes upward to connect the preceding life and the present life of humans, and also to symbolize us marching towards a promising future. I also built simple outlines through burnt tiles with gold foil. In the end, the original appearance of the church was preserved, the building was endued with a new life through the repair of tiles and the hopes of the believers were fulfilled. After this project, I returned to Japan to hold solo exhibitions. The sculptures displayed in galleries were metals featuring the style of installation art. I heated the metals until it became deformed, and then I hung them from the ceiling with fishing lines, creating a dynamic impression as wind blew through. This time in Kaohsiung, I created a sculpture on-site by simply using steel pipes to demonstrate a gradation of shapes and colors through different degrees of oxidation of the material.

Shang Xiao-Feng: In the recent decade, I have been exploring the field of concrete body art in my creation. I value the concept "artists create the spirit, not the forms", or in other words: sculpt the sculpture, not the body. Human body was the reason why I created, not the theme of my artworks. I see human body as an abstract concept, which means "the forms were being created in an abstract way". In the beginning I only managed to copy the forms, however, after continuous work I was able to demonstrate the soul of human body in my sculptures. I integrate the nature of clay with my inner heart and mind. Being trained to learn Abstract Expressionism as I grew up, during the creation process I combined Abstract Expressionism with calligraphy and naturalism. I assume this art style is one of the most important features of Asian artists. I create for myself, not for the public. The same goes with the process of creating public art: the artwork has to be connected with the artist. This time creating at The Pier 2 Art Center was not an exception.

Liang Jen-Hung: Sometimes when I am creating on my own, others will think I look too serious. During the process of creating, my mind is as steady and firm as metal, and this emotion passes on to my artwork. Initially, as I moved from the field of paintings to experiment the creation of artworks with different kinds of materials, I started to think how to demonstrate the "energy" within them. I started to think about the concept of movement. The reason that I thought about "movement" was because that life itself consists of a series of movements. In fact, the whole world can be viewed as a huge energy flow. This concept is in accordance with my interpretation of life which has been displayed through my artworks. It is unpredictable and full of amazing adventures. Fluid dynamics and the simple yet fascinating movement of machines open the audience's microsystem, providing them multi-sensory stimulation. To dominate the nature and the environment, humans carry out measures that have a negative impact on themselves. In response to this situation, I place capsules, which symbolize the negative impact, into the environment in order to demonstrate the fact that the ways humans treat the environment are the same as how they treat themselves.

Human consciousness comes from observations humans have on the details in the environment, such as the flow of wind or minor movements happening in the nature. Showing concern to the nature and maintaining human intellect are equally necessary. I used stainless steel to present the harmonious and positive interaction between humans and the environment; I connect human lives and the energy within the nature in a natural and physically balanced way.

Liu Po-Chun: At the exhibition at Juming Museum in 2004, I built an industrial forest there to highlight the importance of "space". There were eighty steel trees of which the sculpture was built with single overlapping trunks. Centrifugal motors were implemented and changes of green lights were set. I made the trees shiver like birds chirping; I let the audience experience the feeling of an electric shock as they touched the artworks.

As for the exhibition at Tswei-Heng Gallery at Sun Yat-Sen Memorial Hall, I made six strong cows of which six were made from glass fiber with one in white while the other five came in black. Their surface was polished in the end, which looked as bright as the color of a car being baked after painting. They could only move forward or backward on the track. A large mirror of the size of a fifty dollar coin was placed in front of them, with the words "2000, Republic of China" written on the coin. This caused some complaints at that time since in the Chinese way of counting, it was only the 99th year since the Republic of China was established. Furthermore, the sculpture of Mr. Sun Yat-Sen, our nation father, was concaved by way of compression molding with blue LED lights flashing on it. Another key feature was that there was a speaker that could replay the sounds the cows made on the track as well as the sound of the audience speaking. All of these designs respond to the spacial flow within Sun Yat-Sen Memorial Hall. The audience might wondered why the sculpture of our nation father was concaved and they might had posed questions concerning the coin and the track. These questions could all be answered because there was a meaning behind every piece of creation.

Session Two

From Workshop to Art Festival : Art Production, city marketing and Cultural Action.

Time: January 4th, 2015(Sun) 14:00-16:00
Venue: HAM Gallery, Da Yi Warehouse,
  The Pier 2 Art Center, Kaohsiung
Host: Liu Jun-Lan
Interviewees: Zhang Hui-Lan, Lai Yong-Xing,
  Liu Po-Chun, Liang Jen-Hung

Host: We will be discussing about three topics. The first one is: The placeality of art creation camp. We invite the curator and the artists to compare the differences between regional features. Secondly, as a way of art production, we will discuss what the challenges and possibilities of creation camps are. Thirdly, creation camps has been extended to the scale of art festivals, and this involves art promotion and city marketing. How to carry out these policies with art and cultural actions at the same time? Are there any conflicts between them?

Ciaotou Sugar Refinery Station and Bomb Shelters Art Festival

Zhang Hui-Lan: I have participated in creation camps many times as an artist previously. It wasn't until the

event at Ciaotou Sugar Refinery Station that I worked as the curator. In the end of 1999, I held an activity at Ciaotou Sugar Refinery Station. In 2001, I gathered artists formally to share art resources in Kaohsiung and Taipei since I was sponsored by the National Culture and Arts Foundation. The exhibition Sour and Sweet Yeast Fungus moved from Ciaotou to Huashan 1914 Creative Park.

The first art village was the Bomb Shelters Art Festival. To involve both the artists and the visitors in the activity, an election for the chief of village was held and the studios were open to the visitors. Artists created at the small studio in turns, which attracted visitors who were curious about the process of art creation. They encouraged the artists ardently day and night. I opened the studio to introduce "the day of an artist",

and to connect vision and performance arts. The second and third Bomb Shelters Art Festival featured ceramic art. Many artists made vines, while ceramicists used sugar, the local material in Ciaotou, to smolder artworks so as to communicate with artists and visitors from other countries or regions. Cultural interaction was created through various ways, including inviting people to visit Ciaotou and holding the International Theater Festival where people from eighteen different countries were invited. Looking back at these festivals, they revealed that the key factor for local festivals to be successful was to involve the visitors in art promotion. Art does not only concern the artists, but also the audience.

For example, in 2001 a Jap-anese artist used sugar as the material to create traditional Japanese tables, cups and plates. The audience were invited to melt the artwork with coke. Many different types of art were displayed in 2006 in Ciaotou, marking the end of the old generation. Some breakthroughs are as follows: Japanese artists demonstrated the history of the sugar industry between China and Taiwan; artists from Taiwan used local materials to forge steel and metal; Liu Ding-Zan used the half train in the sugar station to make interactive artworks.

Host: The discussion mainly focused on the connection between people and the space. In terms of the space, artists enter the space and communicate with the surrounding, exploring within unknown experiences and spacial memories. In terms of people, artists and the audience build up a relation through artworks. However, comparing the steel sculpture in Kaohsiung with the wood sculpture in Miaoli and the stone carving in Hualian, we can see that the main difference is the material. This is a kind of restriction but also the feature of each art festival.

The Crisis of Sanyi Wood Sculpture and The Origin of Wood Sculpture Workshop

Lai Yong-Xing: Last year, 2014, despite the two-year pause previously, the eighth Sanyi wood sculpture workshop was held. Sanyi wood sculpture once faced problems regarding over development, poor quality performance and mass introduction of artworks from China, with the latter leading to more than eighty percent of the wood sculptures on the street being made in China. The lack of successors was also a serious problem. When I visited Sanyi ten years ago, the youngest wood carver had already reached the age of forty, his sophisticated wood carving skills had no one to succeed. Due to this situation, I invited Mr.

Yang Pei-Chen to hold a camp for passing down wood carving skills to university students. They had been through many obstacles such as living in a hostel in the intense heat of summer and work from eight o'clock in the morning to the afternoon or even until night time. Many amongst them were only freshmen without wood carving experiences. Artists' involvement in workshop is highly valued, because elementary training is the base of art creation. Through the assistance of artists, art development has proceeded and influenced the art industry gradually. Transforming little by little from a confined local workshop to an international workshop, the local government's effort is worthy of recognition.

Host: Sanyi wood sculpture festival is quite special and its characteristic is similar to that of Hualian stone sculpture festival. Promoting and reviving local industries are two purposes the art activities listed as follows are being held: joint exhibitions of wood sculpture, workshop and projects about artists' on-site assistance. However, it is very challenging if Miaoli wood sculpture wants to transform from the level of an arts and crafts activity to a professional art festival.

Review of the Fifth Steel & Iron Art Festival

Liang Jen-Hung: The topic of the fifth Steel & Iron Art festival is "Steely Good", which refers to an accurate

creation style. The demand of the measurement accuracy of the size in metal creation is stricter than that of artworks made from other materials. While carpentry measure in "centimeters", metal cutting measures in a unit smaller than centimeters. To encourage interaction, I invited artists of different age ranges as well as different types of artists such as female artists and poets to participate. No industries provided materials in 2010, so the artists could create without restrictions and their creation style was different from that of the art festivals held in different years as a result. Sound Tree, the artwork of the Korean artist Sung Dong-Hun, had bells hung on the tree, which produces sounds as the wind blew through. Unfortunately, the artwork was moved to another place because the neighbors found the sound annoying. This highlighted the relation between the artworks, the environment and the public. In addition, female artist Huang Pei-Yin created a piece of artwork with stainless washers; female artist Huang Hsiao-Shan made a refined artwork with copper. The artwork I made in front of the warehouse office was called "Refute the Waves II" of which the paddles turned as the wind blew. The challenge I had while creating this artwork was the accuracy. The location was also a challenge as this was my first time creating outside my studio. The artworks created at that time weren't large, but they all represented the passion the artists had towards art. All the artworks will always be displayed at the Pier-2 Art Center.

The Concept of Space and Workshop

Liu Po-Chun: Western workshop blur the boundaries of each region by building up interaction between different areas in different countries. However, this trend has not been emphasized as much as before since it reached its peak in 1997. Generally speaking, in western culture, artists would be informed the characteristics of the space where their artworks will be displayed. This method marks the artists as the focus point. For instance, a workshop taking place in the wild in Romania would require the artists to use natural materials in their creations. Woods as long as ten meters or more were provided by the locals. Artists who do not have previous experiences in creating with raw materials would not be suitable in this case. Artists should be capable of completing artworks even if their creating pattern has changed.

However, at "The Steel & Iron Art Festival" in Kaohsiung, artists couldn't complete the artworks by themselves due to the reason that the sizes were too large to be produced by one person. As a result, the artists played the role of an instructor during the creating process. Through collaborating, the artists and their work teams can produce artworks beyond size restrictions. At the Kaohsiung International Steel & Iron Art Festival 2012- Love, Steel, I took artists to Miaoli steel work to show them the wasted steel. The area next to Penglai Warehouse was assigned as the exhibition area, allowing the artists to inflame their inspiration on-site. Last but not least, forum should be held to present to the audience the heartfelt communication between artists.

Host: From the host team's point of view, workshop is a type of beneficial investment under the global economic crisis at present. High quality artworks can be made under the restriction of space, time and materials. This is more economical than commissioned artwork.

Zhang Hui-Lan: I have a different opinion. Looking from different aspects such as space construction and strategies concerning urban and rural areas, the artists performing in workshop should be selected according to their style. Firstly, I wouldn't set limitations on the materials. Secondly, I value the importance of artists having conversations about art. The strategies carried out by Kaohsiung County Government at that time aimed at integrating resources through art festivals, so "connection" became an important characteristic. In order to be in accordance with the social strategies and activities, female art studios were held for the promotion of Women's Art Association then.

Host : Art festivals have featured enhancing local characteristics. This has stimulated art festivals to spring up, especially in this globalized and integrated world. Nevertheless, political promoting might conflict with the artistic ideal and art activities. Some art festivals nowadays are nothing more than tourist attractions.

Lai Yong-Xing : Speaking of the conflicts that might occur within art festivals, the wood carving festival that has been held for several years stands for a good example. The awarding ceremony of the festival has become a stage for politicians' campaign speech. However, due to sufficient budget, artists come and more collectors and tourists are attracted. The wood carving festival is still rather positive overall.

Liu Po-Chun : The nature of a workshop is similar to that of a performance. The artworks all have some connection with the city. In 2014 I attended the workshop of Busan Biennale, with 35 artists in total. It is said that more than three hundred thousand audience attend the festival every year. The local government see this as a major task in promoting the city. They budget, join traditional local features with the event and boost art into daily life through artworks. The esthetic value has been demonstrated and has had a profound influence on the society and education.

Liang Jen-Hung : I think artwork teams have become a part of cultural property of Kaohsiung City. Due to my experiences in construction and engineering, I apply engineering concepts in the process of creating. It was this characteristic of mine that has enabled me to communicate fluently with the technician. In fact, the process of creating an artwork is complex and takes a long time, different types of creation bring out different kinds of challenges. I would be happy to participate if any exhibitions of multiple materials were to be held in Kaohsiung in the future.

Liu Po-Chun: I would also like to talk about city marketing. About twenty artists were invited to Korea last year, with some journalists from certain countries participating from beginning to end. The journalists' accommodation fee and transport costs were reimbursed. This is obviously a sophisticated city marketing strategy. Information about the festival can be reported first hand and be passed on to the public nationwide.

Host : Apart from art education, art promotion, I believe there are other advantages that can be brought out through holding art festivals in the future. This is an aspect worth thinking, even if there might not be a standard answer. I'll put an end to the forum with this open question. Thank you for your participation.

高雄市政府文化局 策劃　　藝術家 執行

策畫單位 | 高雄市政府文化局
執行單位 | 藝術家出版社
統　　籌 | 史哲
策　　劃 | 劉秀梅　郭添貴　簡美玲
執　　行 | 王慧琳　洪從真　李沅真
發 行 人 | 何政廣
文字編輯 | 張羽芃　陳琬尹
英文翻譯 | 謝汝萱　張羽芃　陳郁棠
美術編輯 | 黃媛婷

出 版 者 | 藝術家出版社
　　　　　　台北市重慶南路一段147號6樓
電　　話 | (02)2371-96923
傳　　真 | (02)2331-7096
郵政劃撥 | 01044798 藝術家雜誌社帳戶

總 經 銷 | 時報文化出版企業股份有限公司
倉　　庫 | 桃園縣龜山鄉萬壽路二段351號
電　　話 | (02)2306-6842

南部區域代理 | 臺南市西門路一段223巷10弄26號
　　　　　　　 | 電話：(06)261-7268
　　　　　　　 | 傳真：(06)263-7698
製版印刷 | 欣佑彩色製版印刷股份有限公司
初　　版 | 2015年09月
定　　價 | 新臺幣380元

ISBN: 978-986-282-160-2（平裝）

國家圖書館出版品預行編目資料

無限上鋼：高雄國際鋼雕藝術節. 2014／
高雄市政府文化局編
-- 初版 -- 臺北市：藝術家，2015.09
160面：28.7×21公分

1.藝文活動　2.雕刻　3.金屬　4.作品集　5.高雄市

733.9/131.4　　　　　　　　　　　104014633